Small Legs, Big Teeth:

A Prequel of Something Yet to Come

Small Legs, Big Teeth:

A Prequel of Something Yet to Come

Kelly Wiesehan

NEW DEGREE PRESS
COPYRIGHT © 2021 KELLY WIESEHAN
All rights reserved.

SMALL LEGS, BIG TEETH:
A Prequel of Something Yet to Come

ISBN   978-1-63676-901-1 *Paperback*
          978-1-63676-965-3 *Kindle Ebook*
          978-1-63730-068-8 *Ebook*

Table of Contents

Introduction   9

Live Free or Die   15

Catholic School & Gorgonzola   29

The Falling in Love Part   45

Yes, and   59

Golden Ticket   71

Stretched Inside Out   83

Small Legs, Big Teeth   99

Black Mold   113

The Saddest Part   129

Ashes to Ashes   137

Friends: A How-to Guide in Process   151

The After-Party: A Spiritual Cocktail   163

A Truly Irish Goodbye   173

My Favorite Day of the Year   187

Acknowledgments   207

To Dad, who made me a storyteller.

To Mom, who made me tough.

To Ryan, who will probably never read this book, but I want everyone else to know that he is the most badass, adventurous, and fearless person I know, and I probably only wrote this book to say that I've done something cool too. Ryan, you are my favorite person. Joke's on you if you never read this.

And to everyone who has ever called me short. I don't believe you.

Introduction

———

"This is the best night of my life!" I yelled up into the rainbow disco balls in the nightclub in Paris. I danced and sang and toasted my drink to Paris! I had finally made it after years of collecting countless Paris posters and little Eiffel Towers in my bedroom.

Little did I know four hours later, I would receive a call from my mother, awakening me from my drunken slumber and yelling at me to book a flight back home to St. Louis because the President issued a European travel ban.

The best night of my life quickly turned into me walking the streets of Paris alone in the middle of the night—still a little tipsy and with only my duffel bag on me—fleeing Europe as Covid-19 was just beginning to wrap its sneaky fingers around the globe.

Two eerie flights, six glasses of wine, and three concerned customs agents later, I dropped my duffel bag on the floor of my childhood bedroom in Imperial, Missouri. Try that for a fun night out!

My eyes darted across the room to the stack of diaries piled on the bottom of my nightstand.

"Woah," I breathed out, exhausted from fleeing back to America, but also from the surreal realization that . . . *I had done it.*

I grew up in Imperial, Missouri. I guess I'm still growing up here because I haven't officially moved out (yet) and my prefrontal cortex isn't fully developed (yet). Imperial, Missouri is exactly what it sounds like. Middle of nowhere. Unimportant. Irrelevant. It is all of these things, including the former meth capital of the world. It's about forty minutes South of St. Louis and is just a random spot in Missouri with one Main Street, a Catholic church, a few trailer parks, and lots of scenic, rolling green hills.

I grew up sitting in my backyard with a diary, furiously wracking my brain for ways to get out of Imperial, make money, and see the world. Because Imperial is extremely boring, dull, and lifeless, I became absolutely infatuated with whatever was the complete and utter opposite.

Fame! Lights! Parties! Dancing!

Every single movie and television show I watched took place in New York City or Los Angeles. *Those must be where the cool and important people are*, I remember thinking. *I have to get there.* I just wanted (want) to be important and have lots of cool friends and a Nicholas Sparks boyfriend like everyone in the movies. Don't we all?

When I came home from studying abroad in Europe, I counted nine diaries stacked on the bottom of my nightstand. They had accumulated over the years and now I was twenty-one. There they were, filled cover to cover with naive pearls of wisdom: my coming-of-age stories. There, in writing, was *proof* of my growing up.

Mistakes. Lessons. Love. Heartbreak. Death. Sex. Religion.

It's all there—unedited, untouched, and undeniable.

I've done it, I thought as I knelt on my floor, wearing the same clothes I wore in Paris twenty-four hours earlier.

I've gotten out. I've seen the world. I've fallen in love—hard—with a Nicholas Sparks boyfriend! I've gotten into a Top 20 University. I've lived in New York City and worked for NBC at 30 Rockefeller Plaza! I've taken out loans and lost all of my money. I've had my heart broken—badly. I've made best friends! I've lost best friends. I've gone to Ireland, Vienna, Budapest, and Paris by myself! I've questioned my upbringing, my values, my beliefs, and everything in between.

I've stopped believing in God. I've had sex. I've done drugs! (Not really though. Sometimes I'll smoke my little brother's weed with him.) I've been to protests. I've started believing in God and Buddha and the Universe and science. I've made my own money. I've worked my ass off! I've come back home to Imperial, Missouri due to a global pandemic, and have lived with my family again—something I wasn't planning on doing, but something I desperately needed.

But I will leave again!

Because I'm only twenty-one, and there's a lot left to do!

I spread out all nine diaries on the floor and started paging through them. Gasping! Laughing! Crying and cringing!

What good are all of these diaries lying on my floor? I thought. *What good are all of these lessons learned and battles won if they can't be shared?*

In the age of social media, where people are posting the highlight reels of their life—vlogging facials, telling you what to buy, who to vote for, what to believe in, what causes to donate to, who to cancel, and curating aspirational, semi-delusional, and potentially insensitive mood boards that make everyone else feel like shit—I'm thinking I can pull back the curtain and show you the real shit.

Because what good is sharing stuff about your life if no one can relate?

When I was having an identity crisis and struggling with heartbreak and losing friends and having a hard time in school, there was no podcast or click-bait YouTube vlog titled "Who Am I? Should I Dump My Boyfriend? Should I Change My Major? Is God Real? Am I Crazy or Is This What Growing Up Feels Like?"

I want to write a coming-of-age story that's happening in real-time. I can't think of a better way to do that than to publish my diary entries and hand over the *proof* I am growing up, making mistakes, questioning things, and trying to have a good-ass time.

Although it is cringeworthy to read my middle school, high school, and even more recent diary entries, I've learned we have to honor our evolution, be open to change, and accept the fact we will always be growing and we will never fit into a singular mold. That's the best fucking part about all of this! If I'm not throwing this book out of the window in five years, something went wrong because I must not have learned anything!

I am not famous and neither are you. (But if you are, that is very cool you are reading this book. Take me with you!) This is not a *New York Times* Bestseller about my extraordinary rich and famous lifestyle. (Not yet, anyway!) This is not an autobiography or a memoir because I am only twenty-one and my story is just revving up. This is not a manifesto where I reveal some crazy life philosophy . . . although I could go there. I'm not here to tell you I've figured it all out. That would be dumb at age twenty-one . . . and boring as hell. I'm here to say: *I know, right?*

This is for everyone growing up and wondering what the hell is going on. This is for people who want to be cool and important like the people in movies, but don't know where to start. This is for people who hear things about feminism and politics from their intellectual friends, but don't know what it means to them yet. This is for people in the build-up before the bass drop.

This is my prequel, and I have no idea what's coming next. Neither do you! How titillating! How nerve-wracking! How exciting!

So let's get this show on the road. In your hands lie my deepest, darkest secrets: my diary entries and some added reflections, of course. Read these secrets wisely, and tell all of your friends.

Peace out,

Kelly Wiesehan

Imperial, Missouri 2020

(P.S. One time, I signed off a cover letter with "peace out". I got an interview the next day.)

Live Free or Die

September 23, 2014

Age 15, sophomore year of high school

It sucks living out here. Nothing ever goes on—ever. And I'm stuck here while kids in Kirkwood walk to each other's houses and all their parents are friends and they all have neighborhood barbeques and shit. They all go to a regular high school like Glee.

But no. I'm stranded in the middle of fucking nowhere, when I could be in New York City at a nightclub meeting crazy people . . . or at least walking to a restaurant with all my friends. Or riding my bike to the park to meet a cute boy or something. No. I can't do those things. Because I live so far away from everything!

Sometimes I just need to escape. My world feels so small— same faces, same places. It's moments of claustrophobia, like now, where I picture myself in a big-ass city with millions of people.

Growing up where I am, everything is so far away from me. And I'm only fifteen; I can't even drive yet. The idea of proximity is almost overwhelmingly exciting to me. The idea of being able to walk to a friend's house or even just a restaurant.... Oh my gosh! I could walk to work too! Wow.

This is why I belong in New York, LA, or even Chicago would do. Possibility lies there! Not to mention, the vast amount of people and parties I could go to. Ah, I just want to be where it all is. You never hear of cool people, parties, and places in Missouri, Kansas, Nebraska, or wherever. Where do you hear about that stuff? New York. LA.

That's where I want to be. Right in the mosh pit of things! Right in the midst of chaos. And I'm willing to walk into that alone if I have to. But the exciting thing is that I'll find people along the way that will be there for me. There's so many people and places waiting to be discovered, and I can't wait to do just that.

So yeah. Sometimes I just need to escape. I'm claustrophobic. I'm suffocating. But it won't last forever.

When I finally get my chance, take a good look at me, because it might be a while before you see me again!

"You've got to be kidding me," I said when God plopped me down on this earth, smack-dab in the middle of nowhere. God laughed that deep, Morgan Freeman belly laugh and *POOF*—He was gone, and I was stuck in Imperial until further notice.

Ah, Imperial, Missouri. Where do I begin? It's a love-hate relationship. Imperial is strange because one moment, you're driving through beautiful tree canopies with incredible views of green hills in the distance, and then you come to a halt at a stop sign and see a yard full of rusted Natural Light cans and a guy in a wife beater smoking a cigarette through his broken screened-in door.

Imperial is about forty minutes South of St. Louis. It's not a cute suburb with sidewalks and tulips and cute little schools kids walk to and from every day. No. It's spread out with long, dirt roads, trailer parks, and old barns converted into meth labs. Contrastingly, weaved into all this are some nice neighborhoods nestled into the hills with majestic, breathtaking views.

Some people make the argument Imperial is peaceful and beautiful; calm and serene; open and filled with nature. My dad fucking loves Imperial. I personally find it dull, isolating, disgusting, and lifeless. The winters are the worst. Everything is dead, brown, gray, and silent. There's nothing to do here—really, there isn't. We have one or two strip malls with an H&R Block, a Great Clips, and one smoky bowling alley that gives you second-hand lung cancer. Oh, and the tanning salon I went to in high school.

I wouldn't even call it a *small town* because that implies a charming and dainty community where everyone is friends and there's a town square where everyone goes to do their shopping. No. Nobody knows each other. We're all spread out, lingering in solitude somewhere in the woods, hoping nobody comes to bother us. That's why people (my parents) move to Imperial—to be alone and unbothered. . . . Or because it's cheap.

I went to a private Catholic grade school from kindergarten to eighth grade with the same twenty-three kids for nine years. I tried hanging out with people from public schools to have more friends, and because they actually had parties on the weekends. But I was rarely invited, despite how desperately I wanted to be.

When I went to high school—which was a thirty-minute drive away—and told people I was from Imperial, they always made weird faces.

"Where is *that*?" They'd scoff and crinkle their nose. One time, a girl asked me if I got different radio stations. I was so embarrassed. But we do in fact have some different ones. My friends in high school lived forty-five minutes away. Sometimes I was excluded from group events simply because I couldn't make it there and back in time for my curfew. I blamed being left out on living so far away from everyone. Even when I had the freedom to drive, Imperial was still trapping me in a tiny bubble.

I grew up sitting in my backyard on the brown, crunchy grass, staring into the abyss, wondering what the rest of the world was doing while I was standing still. The silence was deafening.

But as soon as I stepped foot into my house, chaos ensued. There's nothing dull and lifeless in the Wiesehan home, let's get that straight. It's loud, exciting, rambunctious, expressive, happy, angry, silly: all at once and all the time. It's a constant emotional whiplash—sometimes in a good way, sometimes in a crazy way.

My dad built our house on top of a hill. It's a massive glass box. The house is essentially one big room with three stories of floor-to-ceilings windows–seventy-two to be exact. The rest of the rooms are pushed to the side with catawampus dimensions. At night, my dad presses a button and a fifteen-foot-wide screen propels down from the ceiling and a movie theater erupts into the living room. Next to the projector screen is a stage that's lit from underneath my dad built to host the sparkling white grand piano my grandpa passed down to us.

Across the room is a bar, glistening with suspended gold lights, and a stoned backsplash with pillars on either side of the half-moon granite countertop that spans the entryway of the house. Sunshine bursts through the kitchen, which is a glass dome suspended over the hill, overlooking the Ozark mountains, dotted with black cows in the distance. A balcony curves out above the living room, creating another stage for me to sing and dance (or fight with my parents) through the open space.

My dad built it all; he was the visionary and the executor. He's a creative genius, and his masterpiece has fused its DNA into my family's. "This house is an extension of me! I see myself in every part, and I never want to leave!" He proclaims frequently.

The expansive, open space mimics the lack of boundaries within our family. *Everything* is out in the open, literally and figuratively. This space was designed to house our colossal personalities. This quirky, limitless space left us no choice but to express ourselves to the nth degree.

There's only four of us: Mom, Dad, Kelly, and my younger brother Ryan. But we fill that motherfucker up to the brim with laughing, screaming, crying, singing, and dancing.

There are scales that exist from one to ten. However, ours is broken. The Wiesehans only operate at a level ten. Someone is angry? They're a level ten angry: yelling, shouting, cussing. Someone's sad: they're on the floor, curled up in a ball, heaving sobs. (Actually this is just me.) Someone's happy: a surge of adrenaline hurls them through the house as they profess what a glorious day they are having! It's fantastic and horrible and so much fun all at once.

We all look the same: very short, tiny bodies with pale skin, extremely dark hair, and wickedly bright eyes. That is, until I started dying my hair blonde like every girl wants to do at some point.

My parents are extreme by nature. Everything out of their mouths is hyperbolic, melodramatic, and convincing as hell. My parents started their own coffee business before I was born. It was the first espresso bar in Downtown St. Louis. They gave away lattes and mochas for free in 1995 because nobody knew what they were yet. They slaved one hundred hours a week, fighting to make a penny. After five years, they finally started turning a profit and moved out of my mom's parents' basement and into a house. Then they had a baby: me!

"You kids have no freaking idea how hard your mother and I worked!" My dad would exclaim, usually once a week.

"Yeah!" My mom would chime in. "We were scrubbing floors on our hands and knees, changing soda filters, cleaning out ice cream freezers, and putting out fires from the coffee roaster! We never slept!"

"You will never work a day in your life like your mother and I!" My dad would finish.

"You know, Ryan," I'd lean over to my brother after our parents' weekly performance. "We're gonna be eighty-five and half dead, and we *still* will have never worked a day in our lives." We'd snicker, bonding over the fact crazy people are raising us.

"Fuck that! I'm gonna be a billionaire. Watch me, bitch!" And Ryan would get up and retreat to his room in the basement where he builds bikes, gadgets, and . . . bongs. He is a crazy son-of-a-bitch and I bet he will be a billionaire.

My dad has instilled in my brother and I a sacrosanct, mandatory, and undeniable sense of grit, determination, and vigor. He wants to see us work hard and go even further than he has. He wants us to have an appetite for the world, to be hungry for success. We've grown up being told to do "whatever it fucking takes" to achieve our goals, follow our dreams, and go after what we want boldly and fearlessly, no matter the circumstances.

"Kelly, I swear," my dad started to rev up on one of his motivational lectures. "If you wind up married to some boring guy and move back to St. Louis and become a stay-at-home mom . . . *I will be so disappointed in you!*" he'd shout. He's coming from a place of love, but it always feels like I'm in trouble for . . . having potential, I guess?

My dad has big, crazy, lofty fantasies about the world. He is an emotional story-teller with a theatrical personality. If he'd had the luxury of going to college for whatever he wanted, I bet he would have been an artist or a film major. He's inherently artistically inclined, and it's very obvious I get my charisma and creativity from him.

My mother on the other hand is a stone cold, unemotional, show-me-the-facts kind of woman. There is nothing soft about her, except for when she cries at a OneRepublic song and says the rosary for my lunatic brother, praying he doesn't die doing backflips on his BMX bike. Her world is black and white; something either *is* or it *isn't*. Ironically, she loves the Bible and conspiracy theories.

I always go to my mother when I have dramatic breakdowns. I don't know when I'm going to learn my lesson and stop doing this because she always stares at me with a straight face while I crumble to the ground in heaving sobs.

"I don't know how to fix your problems," she always says.

"I'm not asking you to!" I'll cry back. "Sometimes people just need someone to *listen!* Have you ever heard of *empathy*? Just hug me and lie and say it's going to be okay!"

"Why would I lie?" She'll ponder, truly puzzled. "I guess I don't know what empathy is. Do you want a hug? I'm sorry, I'm not good at this."

At this point, I'll start laughing because seeing a mother lack all of the traditional motherly traits you'd expect her to have is funny to watch. My mother is brutally honest and will always tell anyone how it is, even if they don't want to hear it. *Especially* when they don't want to hear it. She tells people they have cancer for a living. It takes a specific type of person and my mom fits the bill.

But she has made me tough in this way. She's taught me it's not very productive to whine and cry about things that are out of my control. It's much more noble to stand up and keep moving. She wouldn't call it noble, though. She would say it's the only option.

When I was in middle school, my mom decided to go back to school to get her Nurse Practitioner degree while working full time as a nurse. The coffee business was still recovering from the 2008 recession. Times were tight, but my mom was dead set on sending my brother and I to Catholic school. She started her NP program and I hardly saw her for three years: eighth grade to sophomore year of high school. She couldn't have done it without my dad's tenacious motivational speeches pushing her forward, telling her she could do it. She worked twelve-hour days at the hospital, came home, and hibernated in the basement until midnight. My dad cooked her dinner and brought it down there every night, almost like she was a prisoner. It was sad sometimes, but we were all so proud of her.

Watching my mom, forty-three, walk across a stage in a cap and gown was a truly inspirational moment in my life. It showed me it's never too late to go after something you want. It's never too late to pivot. It's never too late to start walking a new path in another direction. You *never* have to be complacent.

Complacency and mediocrity had no place in my vocabulary growing up. I grew up doing competitive cheerleading. Not the kind with pom poms—the kind where they toss you fifteen feet in the air, you do a kick and a twist or two. Maybe someone catches you at the bottom, but sometimes they don't, and you hit the floor and break your ankle, or get a concussion if you're lucky. Then, a forty-year-old gay man screams at you and tells you to get up and do it again, but with a smile next time. Oh, and you're ten years old and wearing a rhinestone sports bra and red lipstick. *That* kind of cheerleading.

I got roped into it accidentally. I was in gymnastics class at age seven, like a lot of young girls are, but of course, I took it very seriously (like my mom) and I was very passionate (like my dad). The first time they told us to do a high kick, I swung my knee right up to my face and almost knocked my teeth out. I bled everywhere. But I was okay, and I wanted to do more! I begged the teachers to show me how to do a backflip, but they said I had to perfect my handstand roll first. Screw a handstand roll—those are boring as hell. I wanted to do *flips*!

My mom drove me to open gym on Saturdays and I ran around the gym, chucking myself backward on all of the mats until I figured out how to do a back hand-spring. After two hours, I was doing them on the floor. I went to gymnastics class the next day and showed my teachers. I got in trouble.

But the cheer coach looked over and saw and suddenly, I was in cheer class instead.

Gymnastics is elegant and calculated; competitive cheer is a kamikaze-inspired glitter war. Gymnasts are poised and have extensive training; cheerleaders aggressively whip, chuck, and fling themselves around. If you're a cheer coach, you can't afford to have scaredy-cat on the team because the things you do in cheer aren't possible if you have even an ounce of fear. I had none.

But there's no such thing as *cheer class*, I came to find out. You're just on the team. Before my mom knew it, we were traveling every weekend to convention centers in Kansas City, Springfield, Chicago, and Dallas. She laced fake ponytails into my scalp and glued silver glitter onto my eyelids. She didn't want to, but the other moms told her she had to. It all happened so fast and before I knew it, I was on a level five cheer team by age twelve. That's the highest level you can be on until you're eighteen and cheer in college.

By thirteen, I had broken my collarbone, gotten two concussions, and sprained my left ankle three times. But who cares? I could do a backflip with two twists in it! The thing about growing up doing competitive cheer, or any competitive sport I imagine, is it instilled in me a drive to win. Because if we didn't win, we were running laps and doing push-ups as punishment for *not* winning.

After the last concussion I received, I told my gym I wasn't traveling out of town for the competition that weekend. The blaring cheer music vibrating through a convention center for seventy-two hours was—*shocker*—not what the doctor ordered. My coaches emailed us back and told me they were moving me down a level: punishment. I quit right after that.

Cheerleading had been my outlet–my escape from Imperial. I loved performing in front of crowds, traveling around the country, and flipping through the air with adrenaline coursing through my veins. It was such a rush. Once I quit, I was yanked right back to my tiny Catholic school bubble. I needed somewhere for that fiery, competitive energy to go, so I channeled it into becoming the best Catholic kid I could. I was conditioned to win.

They aren't messing around when they joke about Catholic guilt, let me tell you. It's real. You think running laps and doing push-ups is bad? Try Hell.

I was a passionately obedient child; I wanted to be told the rules of the game and I wanted to win. When teachers told me I could potentially spend eternity in the fiery grips of Satan if I didn't follow the rules, you bet your ass I believed them! I wanted to follow all of the rules perfectly!

I remember hearing rumors in third and fourth grade that to have a baby, people had to have sex. It was the same time kids were going around saying Santa wasn't real. I didn't like those kids, and always yelled at them for being jerks.

"My parents would never do that," I spat back at my neighbor who was trying to tell me a penis goes inside a vagina.

I thought to have a baby, my parents just hugged in bed and prayed to have one. I guess I'm crazy for thinking I too, along with Jesus Christ, was conceived by the Holy Spirit. There is only one Virgin Mother. And it's my mom.

A few days after my neighbor tried to tell me the truth, I went to go watch TV in my parents' bed. I rolled over and felt something jab me in the back. I reached under the covers and pulled out a pink and purple bottle labeled "Astroglide."

When I pulled out this pink and purple bottle with a clear, slimy liquid inside, my initial thought was, *this is to smooth flyaways in your hair.* I flipped the bottle over to read the directions.

"Take a dime size dollop and place onto genitalia—"

"AGH!" I screamed and threw the bottle across the room and burst into tears. *No! It couldn't be! I thought my parents were good people!*

I felt incredibly betrayed and lied to. This was one of my first losses of innocence—the first pop in my carefully-curated bubble. I didn't talk to my parents for the rest of the day. My mom drove me forty minutes to cheer practice that night and I didn't say a word.

Finally, after cheer practice on the car ride home, my mom asked me what was wrong. I burst into tears again. It had been eating away at me all day. My mom swerved into a go-carts parking lot and threw the car into park.

"What's wrong? Are you okay?" she asked. I could hardly catch my breath. My parents were going to Hell! I couldn't save them!

"I know—" I breathed in between sobs, "I know that you and dad—" I took a deep breath. I could hardly say it out loud. "I know you and dad had *sex!*"

My mom erupted into hysterical laughter. She threw her head back and slapped her hands on the steering wheel, cracking up. I was so confused.

"Kelly!" My mom laughed. "It's okay if you love the person," she tried to explain to me. I was not buying it. That's not what the nuns said in school.

"I thought only famous people did that," I said, remembering all of the songs on the radio explicitly referencing sex and my mom turning it off immediately and lecturing me about how sex is wrong and I would get an STD and die and go to Hell if I ever did that.

She laughed and told me again it was okay if you loved someone and were married. I still didn't buy it. I cried every night for weeks at the thought of my parents going to Hell. Luckily, I've since realized I think they're going to be okay.

After nine slow years, I was finally released from the tiny walls of my Catholic elementary school and was ready to enter St. Louis's famous Catholic high school society. My new all-girl high school, which my mom had attended as well, was thirty minutes away in Kirkwood where cool and important kids lived. I was determined to become a St. Louis socialite with riveting weekend plans and a popular friend group. Little did I know it wouldn't be what it was cracked up to be.

Catholic School
& Gorgonzola

―――

"Oh, cool! So, where did you go to high school?" Asks every person from St. Louis ever.

Where you went to high school is the first question we ask anyone. We're known for our baseball, our toasted raviolis, and our exorbitant amount of Catholic high schools. Every suburb of St. Louis has two or three Catholic grade schools. They're all named after a saint or another term for Mary: St. John's, Immaculate Conception, St. Simon's, and my personal favorite, Our Lady of Sorrows. What a depressing name for an elementary school.

There are twenty-five Catholic high schools in the Greater St. Louis area. Twenty-five. Yes, it's excessive. They are private because they are Catholic, not because they are especially academically rigorous. It's the moral rigor that parents pay for. It might have worked too if I hadn't gone to an extremely liberal college and discovered that in fact, not everyone in the world is Catholic and that it's possible to have sex, be gay, *and* take the Lord's name in vain. Who knew?

When there are too many of the same thing in one place, they all have to stand out somehow. Twenty-five Catholic high schools to choose from! How do you decide? Don't worry! I have compiled a list of some of the all-boy and all-girl schools so that you can catch a sneak peek into this bubble.

Unfortunately, my list cannot be exhaustive because I only interacted with a few of these schools, and quite frankly, we don't have time to get to all of them anyway. But what I do know is correct. If by chance you are from St. Louis and you find this list offensive, don't worry—I do too, which is why I have respectively chosen to change the names of the schools. Well, that and I would probably get sued if I didn't.

St. Louis Catholic High Schools, According to Kelly:

All-Boy Schools

The One with Smart Boys: You should go here if you are a nerd and want to go to University of Notre Dame for college. Every boy in St. Louis with red hair attends this school. Notable alumni include Sacajawea's son, my brother, and my ex-boyfriend. The majority demographic consists of primarily Anthony Michael Halls from *The Breakfast Club*. If you have a name that sounds like Kevin O'Keefe, Jack McGregor, or Michael O'Malley, then this is the place for you.

The One with Cute Boys: You should go here if you play lacrosse, have long hair and an Oedipus complex, and drive a Jeep Wrangler to school. Every boy has an unfortunate vocal fry and an unshakeable belief that Saturday's are "for the boys". Wearing Sperry's and pretending to be good at golf and smoking weed are non-negotiable. If you keep your sunglasses on at inappropriate times and your dream is to be in a fraternity at an SEC school and get a lot of pussy and alcohol poisoning, then this is the place for you.

The One with Athletic Boys: You should go here if you want a minimum of three concussions from playing sports and are willing to lose brain cells over it.

The One with Rich Boys: You probably don't want to go here but your father is a cardiologist and has to send you to the best high school in the world in order to nurture his massive ego. Your mother stays at home. You will go to school from 7 am to 5 pm, be forced to play a varsity sport, and be taught by British monks. I didn't know Catholics had monks, but apparently, we do. Have fun and I'm sorry.

The One with (Extra) Preppy Boys: Notable alumni include someone who is in the NBA now but I forgot his name because I'm short, so why would I know anything about basketball? If you care about getting a good ACT score, learning how to grill a nice steak, belonging to a country club, and going to a private college to study finance, then this is the place for you.

All-Girl Schools

The One with Nice Girls: You should go here if you are smart, don't care about being popular, work really hard, and want to make incredible life-long friends. If you don't know how to do your makeup, then this is the place for you. I should have gone here, but I was too good at makeup and making bad friends.

The One with Hot Girls: You should go here if you are into playing club sports and are one of those hot girls that plays soccer. Alex Cooper, the host of the *Call Her Daddy Podcast*, would have gone here. If you are interested in underage drinking, going to Texas Christian University, and getting a brand-new BMW on your sixteenth birthday, then this is the place for you.

The One with Edgy Girls: You should go here if you consider yourself an artist, a theater kid, or a poet. They believe that God is a woman and somehow manage to feel sexually empowered despite being told that premarital sex is a mortal sin. I don't know how this happens. It is home to two types of people: those who sketch cartoons and dye their hair blue and those that do cocaine in an unfinished basement at age seventeen. Ideally, you are both of these simultaneously.

The One with Basic Girls: You should go here if your mother wishes she was on *Dance Moms,* is a functioning alcoholic that drives a Lexus SUV with a Louis Vuitton purse in the passenger seat at all times, and still talks about her college sorority. You will probably go here if your grandmother, mom, and sister also went here because if not for a legacy, there really is no appeal besides joining the sexy dance team. Everything you own is monogrammed. If you want to roll up your plaid skirt, drink UV Blue from the bottle on the weekends, and have a membership for spray tans, then this is the place for you. I went here.

The One with High Society Girls: Go here if dressing up in a wedding gown and doing a Virgin Pagan ceremony at the end of your senior year sounds fun. If that made any sense, then this is the place for you.

After what felt like being held hostage in my tiny Catholic grade school with the same twenty-three kids for nine years, I was eager to burst into high school and meet as many people as possible. At the same time, my distaste for Imperial was only growing, and I was desperate to be *popular* like the girls in the movies. Not because I wanted to be well-known, per se; I just wanted to go to parties!

My high school was thirty minutes from Imperial and the girls that went there were from *fancy* suburbs of St. Louis like Kirkwood and Des Peres. They went to *cool* Catholic elementary schools that had always beaten us in sports and actually had cute boys and mixers on the weekends.

I wanted to be friends with *these* girls. I wanted the social life that they had, or at least the social life that it *looked like* they had on their Instagrams, which I followed before I even got to school so that when I arrived, I knew exactly who to network with. I was on a mission. I now know that this behavior is called "social climbing", and it usually never ends well.

But alas! Everything went according to plan! I went to a summer field hockey camp before my freshman year, identified my targets, made some small talk with them, and by the end of the camp, they had invited me to the Back-to-School Mixer at the School with Smart Boys that happened during the first week of school.

I was ecstatic! I had a friend group! I had somewhere to be on the weekends! And I was meeting all of their *cute guy friends* from their *cool* elementary schools at *mixers* and *football games!*

But things eventually turned south. Stories involving *popular girls* rarely end well, in my experience. Making friends solely on the basis of how I thought they could enhance my social life was first, manipulative and wrong, and second, just plain stupid. By my sophomore year, I was getting nervous that I had made a mistake.

January 8, 2015

Age 16, sophomore year of high school

No one is willing to be vulnerable and put themselves out there. No one is willing to give. We just sit in silence at the lunch table, texting each other under the table. And we pretend to be friends, secrets holding us together. We're fucking afraid of each other, honestly.

We aren't nice. It kills me. I was in it before I knew. I just wanted to have a big group of friends like they show on TV. I wanted to have plans on the weekends! I didn't know it would turn out to be so . . . hollow.

No one goes out of their way to do anything nice. All it takes is a two second text to invite that one extra person to the party and make someone feel included. Our friend group doesn't know how to do that.

I played a game at sophomore retreat where Terri Hyat, our Campus Minister (someone who is in charge of making us do religious activities, I guess?) called out a topic and we went to the designated station in the gym that matched what we believed. "Favorite subject in school: Math is station one, English is station two! Go!" And we all ran around the gym to find the station that matched what we agreed with.

Not one of my friends wound up at any of the same stations as me. But I was around the same people amongst my many stations. Shouldn't those be the people I hang out with?

It sucks to realize that when you're already in too deep. That's high school: everyone running to the place they want to be, not the place they're meant to be. But I guess no one knows who they're meant to be. Anyway, it's all trial and error, dipping your toe into the water.

You know when you take something from a buffet, try it, and hate it? You can't really put it back on the serving tray with a bite out of it. (Or can you?) So, you reluctantly keep it on your plate. And that's where I am: stuck on a plate.

I was not exempt or innocent from the toxic behavior that ensued in this friend group. The things that made it toxic were things a lot of young girls will always do. We talked bad about everyone behind their back. We were jealous of each other. We never wanted to celebrate someone's success because we always felt threatened by one another. We upheld unspoken rules about how to dress, what to look like, what kinds of jokes to make.

If someone slipped up, they were getting an eye roll and a nasty text message sent about them under the lunch table. And the worst part: we thought we were really, *really* fucking cool.

I've reconnected with a lot of these girls, and we see clearly now that we had gotten it all wrong. Individually, we're all good people with unique aspirations, hobbies, and passions. But we never talked about those things in high school. We were too busy trying to fit in with each other. Our grade only had ninety girls. Every week, we'd hear about a girl from one friend group getting kicked out, and we'd watch her move lunch tables the next day– all ninety pairs of eyes on her.

My friend group was *mean*. If we were going to be kicked out, it would have been vicious. So we conformed and behaved. We needed the security of thinking we were cool and had an actual friend group, or at least people to sit with at lunch, because deep down I think we were all insecure. Well, I know I was at least, and insecure people do desperate things to fit in, like talk shit on their best friend because everyone else is doing it.

Let's circle back to the lunch table. The thing about this lunch table is that it was *really* squished into the back corner of the cafeteria. So if you didn't get to the lunch table first, you'd have to crawl over everyone to get to the chairs in the back corner.

You know how when you slide into a church pew, you slide all the way to the other side? Or if not a church pew, into an Uber, for example, so that the person behind you doesn't have to crawl over you? It's called basic human decency. Well, every day at lunch time, my friend group sprinted to our lunch table in order to secure a chair that was *not* squished into the back corner. The first girls to arrive snatched the easy-access chairs that could be scooted in and out very freely. What luxury.

I am very short. *How does this relate*, you ask? I have a point. Being short means that, relatively, I have a farther distance to travel. My legs are tiny. Although I appear to be power walking, I am moving at a very average walking pace. This resulted in me being the last girl to lunch every single day. All of the open, freely-scootable chairs were already taken.

Every day, I climbed over these girls every with my massive Kate Spade purse, heavy textbooks, and my lame Velcro lunch box with my soggy turkey sandwich inside. There was hardly enough room between the back of the chair and the table to not get your arms get stuck. God forbid you had to pee or forgot to get ketchup. You were stuck there. One day, I finally lost it.

"Okay, why on Earth, if you get here first, would you *not* take the furthest seats!" I yelled at the seven doe-eyed girls. "It's like sliding into a booth at a restaurant and just stopping and not scooting over for the person behind you. Do you *get* that? It's the same principle! It's so rude!" I threw my hands in the air as I stood on my chair. (You had to stand on it before you sat down, because you didn't have floor access!) Everyone looked at me silently and I sat down in my squished chair, out of breath and embarrassed.

No one said anything, and then everyone looked down, pulled their phones out, and started texting and smirking. I sat there, assuming they were making fun of my outburst over iMessage.

We sat at this lunch table in silence every day, scared to say the wrong thing. Sometimes two girls had a conversation and the rest of us would just listen, perhaps taking mental notes on what they thought was funny and worth talking about.

"Haha, yeah, totally. I thought that was *so weird* too!" I would try to chime in. The two girls' faces would go stark instantly.

"Wait. . . . What the fuck?" One girl would say, squinting her face, aghast that someone else had spoken.

"Yeah, wait, *what*?" The second girl would laugh with the first girl, securing her spot at the party that weekend.

I remember that I didn't speak very much, afraid of the inevitable eye roll I usually received. I would look over and see the girls from my honors classes laughing and wish I could go over there and stay forever. But I didn't want to make a scene and get uninvited from all future parties. What a coward I was.

When I went to college, I was fascinated by how free I felt to say whatever I wanted. I didn't realize how truly trapped I had felt. These days, I can't seem to shut up!

I remember a particular day at the squished, back corner lunch table. People were texting under the table and talking shit, as we usually did after a painful confrontation. Someone was caught hanging out with someone else's crush that weekend, and we all knew about it. The awkward silence was unbearable and I felt the need to break it up with something lighthearted and silly. So, in typical Kelly fashion, I chirped up and said something annoying.

"Let's go around and all say our favorite cheeses!" I smiled over my turkey and mayonnaise sandwich.

"Okay, you go first," Poker Face said. She always had a deadpan expression.

"Okay! Mine is gorgonzola," I said proudly. Looking back, I think I only brought this up because I had recently discovered that there were *other cheeses* besides American, Swiss, and Cheddar. My intuition told me that knowing a variety of cheeses was a fancy thing to do, and I wanted to appear fancy to my friends. After all, their moms had real Louis Vuitton purses and luxury SUVs.

"I fucking hate gorgonzola," Poker Face said. And that was the end of that game.

Between lunch table drama and psychological warfare, we still went out on the weekends and had a good time. We hung out with a group of boys from the School with Cute Boys, and my best friend Sabrina threw massive ragers in her basement because her dad let us. I could recount the tales of these massive ragers and tell you all the stories about boys throwing deck furniture into the woods, throwing beer cans into TVs, punching holes in the walls, and smoking cigars in the kitchen and throwing back Everclear shots. But I won't bore you!

I started to have a crush on one of these boys. I won't disclose his name, but I believe he is currently a football player at an SEC school. I'm not sure though. The point is, he's huge and doesn't speak much. But at the time, I thought he was hot and found his dull personality to be quirky and endearing.

One night, at one of these massive ragers, Football Player and I kissed–made out, actually–and I became unglued! I was so excited! I told *everyone* the next day! And the day after that! And then, BAM. In my mind, we had *a thing*. *A thing* is when you're not dating someone and you're not exclusive, but you're also off-limits to anyone else . . . at least in *my* head.

"Wow, he's so funny. I like him *so* much. This might really turn into something!" I'd ramble giddily to my friends. They gave me uncomfortable stares and never responded. I didn't know why.

In August, my friend group went on a mission trip to Appalachia, Kentucky to help rebuild homes. (This may seem off brand for a group of mean girls, but we did go to Catholic school and were required to do acts of service such as this.) It was a great experience, and we really did build a few homes. I was on top of a roof drilling in metal sheets all day, and met a lot of people within the community. But sadly, my mind was preoccupied because Football Player hadn't been answering my Snapchats and I was worried.

One day on a break from working, I went over to a swing set with Poker Face and started swinging. I sensed some awkward tension. She laughed nervously and then stopped swinging.

"Kelly, . . ." she said shakily. "I have to tell you something." My heart stopped. This was out of character for Poker Face. She got up and motioned for me to come sit with her on a bench nearby. I sat down and pretended to be super chill and confident, but I was nervous as hell. She stared at the ground.

"So," she started, her hands trembling, "I've been hooking up with [Football Player] and he told me that he likes me instead of you and he wants to have *a thing* with me, but not you. And I just thought you should know that I think I really like him—Sorry," she blurted out, then looked up at me with big, expectant eyes.

A train ran through my chest. Rejection. Insecurity. Embarrassment. Anger rose in my stomach and I felt my face get hot and my heart start to pound and my throat get tight. I thought about going off on her and making a scene and asserting my dominance and then–

"Oh, I know," I heard the words come out of my mouth calmly. "I figured as much."

I don't know what came over me in that moment, but thank God. I had to sleep in a bunk bed with her for two more days! Making a scene wouldn't have served either of us well. I later FaceTimed her and told her what an awful person I thought she was, and then she went on to date Football Player for two years.

"I told her! She's fine, she doesn't care!" Poker Face announced to my friends as we walked back inside the schoolhouse we were staying at. I don't know if she knew I was right behind her or not, but it was weird as shit. All of my friends had known about this the entire time and had just been watching me pour my soul out over this boy for months. No wonder they weren't indulging my giddy rants!

Instead of feeling sorry for myself, I noticed this wave of adrenaline wash over me. She had screwed me over and was in the wrong. *I was right.* My friends agreed! I was going to hold my head high and sit up even taller on my moral high horse.

I asked my friend Irena—who, to this day, is the sexiest woman I have ever met—to take me to the Bebe store in the mall and pick out tight dresses for me to wear at boy school dances in the fall so that I could show everyone that I could be hot if I tried! And that I could get another boy in a heartbeat!

I'm not sure if this narcissistic coping mechanism is much healthier than crying, feeling sorry for myself, and doing the "why *her* over *me*" thing, but this route was much more exciting and included makeup and new clothes. I spent the rest of the summer going to country concerts in my new clothes and posting hot Instagram photos for all of my potential new suitors to see. These days, people call those kinds of photos "thirst traps".

But by beginning of junior year, I was fed up with the petty girl drama that ensued every day at the lunch table. I complained to my mom every day about the relentless soap opera that was consuming my life. I wanted a way out; I was over it.

"Get a boyfriend and hang out with him instead," my mom said bluntly in the car.

I was shocked. I think a part of me thought I wasn't allowed to have a boyfriend. My dad had told me my entire life to never have a boyfriend because all men are pigs and will lie and say anything to get in my pants.

"You're too strong and independent," he'd say to me in the car. "You don't need a boyfriend. You're so talented and have better things to do!" He wanted me to stay away from boys, like most dads do, and lifting me up onto a pedestal was an effective tactic for a long time.

But all it took was an ounce of approval from my mom and *BAM!* Just as I did in the beginning of high school, I quickly strategized a new mission: acquire boyfriend.

I met him two weeks later and we dated for nearly four years. He was the perfect excuse to not hang out with my hellish friends on the weekends. He happened to be cute, nice, and live close to my school *and* my job at the European Wax Center, which meant less driving time for me! We worked perfectly because I loved hearing myself talk and he had no opinions and a good listening face. It was fantastic.

The Falling in Love Part

———

June 22, 2014:

Age 15, summer before sophomore year of High School

I always say I'll never have a boyfriend in high school. But that relationship is almost like a rite of passage or coming of age type of thing.

I guess what I'm really nervous about is texting someone every day and getting bored . . . and having an actual boyfriend. I never want to be one of those girls. "Kelly as in Jack's girlfriend?" No, that can't be me. I love my independence too much.

Well, it's going to have to be me one day. Maybe just not now.

Having said that, if I ever do date anyone, it better be worth it. I better learn something, become a better, wiser person once it's said and done.

A year after that entry, I threw away that sentiment and was on a mission to find a boyfriend!

I decided a boy with a good handshake would make a good boyfriend. If a boy has a good handshake, it means he probably has a good dad or some father figure in his life who taught him how to not be a dead fish and look people in the eyes with confidence.

This was my logic the night of August 30, 2015, when I went to a backyard party with my high school friends and my best guy friends, Max and Joe Bopp, twins who went to the School with Smart Boys. I had been friends with Max and Joe for a while, but I hadn't met the rest of their friends. This was a networking event, and I came prepared to shake a lot of hands.

The backyard was teeming with boys I had never met before. If you remember anything about these boys from what I've told you, it's they were the smart, nerdy ones. This was perfect for me because I was looking for someone innocent and endearing, someone I could trust not to lie to me just to get into my pants.

I looked up at Joe as we walked into the backyard together.

"I'm going to go and introduce myself to every single boy here and shake their hand," I said. He laughed and cocked his head to the side, confused. "If they have a good handshake, then they are not only smart, but confident as well. Watch."

I went around with Joe shamelessly introducing myself to drunk teenaged boys who, unsurprisingly, had dead fish handshakes. A dead fish handshake is the gross kind where they barely grasp your hand, maybe only your fingers—perhaps because you're a girl and they think you're fragile and don't want to hurt you.

Maybe they're trying to be polite, but why? Do they really think their big, strong hand is going to break my teeny, tiny hand? *Come on.* I can handle a firm, death grip handshake! I know I don't look like a hot thirty-four-year-old six-foot-two-inch male CEO, but I sure as hell feel like one, and I hate when I'm met with a dead fish handshake.

I was starting to feel a little bit hopeless and bored walking around the backyard looking for candidates. Then I saw him: sun-kissed, long, curly hair; wide, tan shoulders. Stumbling and drunk, he crashed into a girl from my high school whose locker reeked of weed because she famously ate edibles in the morning before class. He bulldozed into her and they started making out.

"Oh, woah!" I laughed. I was in the middle of talking to another boy and we started laughing and making fun of them. Joe came over to us and saw what was happening.

"Oh, yeah," Joe chuckled. "That's Yes Man."

His name isn't actually Yes Man, but that's what we will call him. You see, he couldn't say no to anyone, especially me. This was his greatest strength and also his biggest weakness: his rise to prominence *and* his demise.

When Yes Man was done locking lips with Weed Locker, I decided it would be fun to shake his hand—mostly just to mess with him, but also because I kind of liked his surfer dude hair. It reminded me of YouTuber Jay Alvarrez, who was very relevant at the time. I walked up behind him and tapped him on the shoulder. He spun around, eyes red and glossed over.

"Hi, I'm Kelly!" I smiled and shoved my hand out at him. He grabbed it instantly.

"What's up." He laughed and told me his name. His smile sent unexpected butterflies through me. His handshake, despite him being clearly intoxicated and perhaps under the influence as well, was impeccable.

His hand gripped mine firmly, tightly, and confidently. He shook my hand like I was a hot, tall CEO. It was perfect. I was stunned. I thought for sure he had been a dead fish, given his sloppy rendezvous with Weed Locker. But it was the best handshake of the night.

I wound up driving the Bopps and Yes Man to Steak n' Shake after the party. I found Yes Man very silly as he slurred his words to the waitress and earnestly asked for honey mustard for his chicken strips. I sat next to him and we joked and laughed the whole time, ignoring everyone else.

My friends and I went back to a house where the Bopps and their friends were hanging out. I immediately went and sat down next to Yes Man. Our legs touched and it was electric. I was so drawn to him, and to this day I don't know why. He wasn't necessarily "my type." He was also drunkenly flailing about like a clown, but there was something *endearing* about him. *Unassuming.* I just felt this pull to be around him.

I got his Snapchat and we began exchanging funny quips here and there throughout the day at our respective Catholic boy and girl high schools. Meanwhile, I was hanging out with another boy who I had met that same night. Ironically, on my awkward date with the other boy, I couldn't stop asking about Yes Man. I knew they were friends and I wanted to know more.

"Wait, so do you play soccer with Yes Man?" I asked as I stuck a fork into my Qdoba bowl.

"Um, no. He's on Varsity, actually," the boy responded, awkwardly taking a bite from his bowl.

"Do you have any classes with him?" I pressed on.

"Ah, no not really. He's in all honor classes," his voice trailed off and his eyes stayed on his food. I felt bad for asking, but my heart jumped a little bit at the good news. *Varsity and honors classes! Score!*

I continued surveying Yes Man's reputation, asking the Bopps and other girls at my high school who knew him. As it turned out, Yes Man was actually incredibly smart—like genius level—and on the Varsity soccer team and Varsity water polo team. Oh! And he was working on becoming an Eagle Scout. *Boy Scouts and water polo, are you kidding me?* Innocent, endearing. *Check, check.*

In October 2015, Joe Bopp asked his lunch table who the boys were bringing to their Fall Ball dance. Yes Man said he would like to bring me. Joe was originally supposed to bring me, but he told Yes Man to ask me anyway. By that point, we were fervently texting each other excessively long paragraphs throughout the day.

"I have good and bad news," Joe texted me later that day. "I can't bring you to the dance . . . but someone else is interested."

I blushed in the kitchen as I read it. I knew what he meant. I didn't realize how big I was smiling until my dad walked in.

"Oh, no," my dad said across the kitchen counter. "That's that *look*!" he teased.

"What?" I gasped, holding my phone to my chest.

"Dammit," my dad laughed. "Who's the boy?"

"*Nobody!*" I shouted back and ran up to my room to call Joe and ask for all of the details. I was ecstatic.

Yes Man asked me in person that weekend after his soccer game that I went to. We went to the dance together, and luckily, all of my friends from school were invited too. During the dance, Yes Man sneaked away to the bathroom to take edibles, which I thought was weird, but I ignored it. The Boy Scouts and the "being smart" thing counterbalanced it for me. When we got to the after-party, he pulled me into a hug and—*sparks*. I literally remember my eyes bulging and feeling like *woah*. He was suave.

But right as it happened, my friend Sabrina, a ring-leader of my friend group, interrupted.

"Get your stuff. We're leaving right now," she said, slinging her purse over her shoulder and heading for the stairs. I didn't move. "Come on. I'm your ride; let's go. This party is dead. We're going somewhere else."

I looked up at Yes Man. His soft, almond shaped eyes looked disappointed. "I guess I have to go. . . ." I trailed off. I picked up my purse and followed Sabrina up the stairs like a sad puppy. It sucked. I really wanted to hang out with Yes Man. A few other friends of mine piled into the backseat of Sabrina's car, all of us confused and kind of bummed out.

"Where are we going?" Irena asked.

"A different party," Sabrina said, shifting her dad's convertible into gear and taking off. We wound up at some thirty-year-old guy's house who was having a casual get together with his friends . . . who were also thirty. We were sixteen. It was weird as fuck. We walked into this man's house wearing our high school dance dresses and heels. Everyone in the house stopped and gawked at us.

"Jason!" A girl shouted. "Why the FUCK are there sixteen-year-old girls here? You creep!" She yelled over her wine glass. She and her friends started yelling at whoever Jason was and other guys continued talking and drinking beer, ignoring us. Sabrina walked into the kitchen and poured herself a drink. I grabbed Irena and Poker Face and pulled them into a bedroom.

"We gotta get out of here," I said urgently. "Like, why are we here? What the fuck?" My heart was pounding. I had this sickening feeling in my stomach. This situation was so wrong, and we needed to get out.

"There's this app called Uber I've heard of, but I don't think it will come here," Poker Face said. Indeed. Uber had just came out, but not to the St. Louis suburbs. I called Max Bopp and asked if he would come pick us up. I sent him my location. He was thirty minutes away, but he started driving.

I grabbed Irena and Poker Face and we snuck out the front door, still wearing our Bebe dresses and six-inch heels. We started walking on the side of the road. It was thirty degrees outside. I bet we walked over three miles. Max picked us up in a strip mall parking lot. It was two in the morning at this point.

"Get in! Are you guys okay?" Max asked, so concerned. I got in the front seat. I was happy to see him, but so pissed off at Sabrina. That was the last straw for me. I was getting a boyfriend and getting the hell out of these weird antics that happened all too often with Sabrina.

"I guess you guys can just sleep in the basement with us, and I'll drive you home tomorrow morning." Max drove us to where all of the boys were sleeping. I realized Yes Man would be there. I got butterflies and forgot about trudging on the side of the road in stilettos in the middle of the night. I couldn't wait to see him.

My friends and I quietly snuck into the basement where all of the boys were passed out. Yes Man woke up and rubbed his eyes. "Kelly? Oh!" He got up off the floor and walked up to me. "Hey." He rubbed his eyes again, clearly trying to wake himself up. It was almost three now. "Wanna um . . . play cards?"

"Sure," I laughed, confused. Irena and Poker Face snickered and went to go sleep on a couch. All the boys were still passed out. Yes Man walked to the back of the basement, pulled out a deck of cards, and sat down at a table. We played Go Fish for about five minutes and then he flashed his eyes up at me and put his cards down.

"We don't really wanna be playing cards right now, do we?" He smirked. It threw me off! Was he really being so forward? This was awesome! Boys had never been so upfront with me!

"No, I guess not," I whispered, blushing. Yes Man walked over to a random door and opened it.

"Come on," he whispered. I walked over. I could hear Irena and Poker face quietly giggling. I walked in and Yes Man shut the door. It was pitch black. He started laughing. "Oh whoops! This is a storage closet. Guess we're setting up camp here."

He turned the flashlight on his phone on, and there were floor-to-ceiling shelves of camping gear all around us. He grabbed a sleeping bag from a shelf and laid it out on the little patch of concrete at our feet.

We sat down slowly and awkwardly, the sleeping bag crinkling under us. It was dark. We had been texting each other every day for two months at this point. It was obvious we liked each other a lot, but we hadn't been alone in a storage closet yet. The air was tingly with excitement. He sat down next to me and I felt that electric pull again. It felt so nice just to be *near him.*

"I guess . . . this will be our first kiss," I said bashfully. We both laughed, and I grabbed the side of his face and kissed him. It definitely wasn't the best kiss of my entire life. It was an awkward-teenagers-in a-closet-at-three-in-the-morning kind of kiss. But it felt right, and I could feel something new had started.

We hung out two more times after, and on our third date, as we sat in the backseat of his car in a random cul-de-sac making out, he popped the question. It was October 30, 2015.

"I've been meaning to ask you something," he said slowly.

"I won't have sex with you!" I said defensively, scooting away from him.

"What? No," he laughed. "I was wondering . . . if you think we should be boyfriend and girlfriend?"

The car went silent. I was shocked. This was only our third time hanging out. I had flings with guys for eight months straight and never wanted to be their girlfriend.

But there was something about Yes Man I trusted. There was something between us that made the air feel tingly and magnetic and it felt right. We clicked. I took a deep breath.

He had warm, golden eyes and a sweet smile with sharp dimples. Light from a lamp post illuminated his long, golden hair. He looked at me so earnestly. *Endearing. Unassuming.*

"Yes," I breathed out, like I was surrendering, remembering a year earlier when I vowed to never have a boyfriend in high school. But I liked him so much, and I knew there was no going back.

And off we went into the deep end! Not looking over the edge before we jumped.

We drove around St. Louis every single weekend, going on fun dates and holding hands and kissing and doing all of the things. We lived in a bubble together where we had time to have picnics in Forest Park in the morning, a three-hour-long binge-fest of *Friends* in the afternoon, an hour of playing outside with his dog and siblings, a cozy pizza restaurant for dinner, and we'd stop by one of his friends' houses at night to have a few beers. Then we'd go back to his house and watch a movie and cuddle and stare at each other with stupid smiles, and I'd drive home around midnight.

Those days are still some of my happiest days. We had *time* to do that, and it felt like a dream, especially knowing now how busy life gets. I can't imagine the next time in my life when I'm going to have time to fuck around and do that kind of sappy shit all day. Maybe after I move to a new city, get a job, some more friends, go drinking and dancing a lot, write ten more books, start fifty-two businesses, win seven Oscars, burn out, and am ready to settle down at age seventy. Maybe *then*.

But damn. . . . It was so nice while it lasted.

"Wow, every time we hang out, I think I like you even more," I mused one day as we lay in his car with the backseats folded down. We were in an old church parking lot. That's where we went to kiss when his family was home.

"Oh yeah, me too," he said. "It's almost like we're . . ."

"NO!" I stopped him. "Don't say it!" But I knew what he meant, and I felt it too.

November 27, 2015

Age 16, junior year of high school

We were lying on the couch and it just hit me. Silent tears welled up in my eyes and rolled gently down my face. It was overwhelming. So overwhelming.

"This is so much," I breathed on his arm, which was wrapped around me.

"What?" he panicked.

"Nothing. I don't know. It's just a lot all at once, I guess." My eyes stayed glued to the TV, not daring to look at him again, scared I might cry or something. I could feel my walls slowly rising up to block out all sense of emotion, feeling, sensitivity, vulnerability, or whatever other sentimental crap lies down there.

*But I had to stop myself. What, am I really gonna go back
to the way things were before I met him? I can't even imagine. I don't ever want to go back to life before this.*

*I feel so alive, so awake, so present, yet always in a trance.
The world is just a better place with him.*

We fell in love hard and fast. It's a little uncomfortable
to write about now, years later, knowing what I know
now about *love* or whatever, and knowing we were so
young and naive, and knowing this will probably happen
to me again, which is scary. But it was fairytale teenager
love. It was real, and it was amazing.

It felt like *falling*, like letting go and giving up control. There were all these strong emotions and you don't
know what was going to happen. It also *physically* felt like
falling. I swear to God, my stomach was dropping like I
was on a roller coaster with big drops and breathtaking
moments and adrenaline rushes and giddy smiles and
dumb giggles. It was a rose-colored universe. It really
was a trance. It felt like we were the only two people in
the world for over three years.

Being in love feels like walking in Candy Land. Suddenly, the bare, brown, dead trees are pretty. The cold
weather is warm. Old songs from the fifties are really
beautiful and romantic instead of boring and outdated.
Bad days are still good because they end in a tight hug
and an "I love you".

We worked so well together. I talked and talked
and he nodded and smiled. I loved who I was around
him. We were fun and we laughed and we joked and we

played. He never said much, but it was okay. I was dominant and flashy and he was humble and sweet. I was very uptight and he was carefree. He never complained or said no to anything. In fact, he never said much at all. But I never noticed because I was talking and having a wonderful time.

December 19, 2015

Age 16, junior year of high school

"It's crazy to think about because I'm sixteen years old; I mean, I'm so young. Like, this is it? It's almost disappointing to think about. We've got our whole lives ahead of us and I'd like to be alone and do my own thing and be a free spirit and what not, but I can't imagine a day without you..."

He looked at me with that look on his face. The corners of his mouth squeezed the lines on his cheeks that kind of resemble dimples, but sharper than that. It was dark, but his face was flush, and his eyes may or may not have been teary. He let out a sort of laugh.

"I love you so much . . ." he said softly. "But that's a talk for another day." I rambled some more, but my mom came out in the garage and made us come inside. But really, it's crazy.

I want to go to New York and be a sexy businesswoman, and go to Spain and be an artist, and go to Hawaii and be a simple surfer person, and go to Hollywood and walk red carpets. I guess he could do it all with me, but life is so long. There's so many people. There's no way.

I firmly believe there is more than one perfect person for everyone out there. I think if he and I were to be together forever, it would be just fine and I would be happy. But life goes on, the journey continues, and people come and go.

But whenever the time comes around to settle down and tie the knot, someone will be there. It may or may not be him, but I hope it's someone who makes me feel this way, because it's a feeling I don't think I could live without.

Yes, and

———

The best thing you can be is funny. Everyone will like you if you're funny, and it won't matter how short you are. If you can make people laugh, you are more than just a basic white girl with an unnecessary skincare routine. A funny person is an interesting person who people will listen to and actually enjoy.

Since birth, I have been playing dress up and make believe like it's nobody's business. When I was five, I would go into my mom's closet and twist and tie her shirts into extravagant dresses for myself and dance around the house in her high heels. When I was ten, I dressed up as Dolly Parton for Halloween, stuffed my mom's bra with a ton of socks, put on a blonde wig, and received questionable looks from the parents. When I was twelve, I put two rolls of toilet paper in a tube top, drum sticks in my hair, and filmed *Saturday Night Live* spin offs with my friends where I was a recurring character named Nubby (I don't know why) who would join my friends as the guest for the "Weekend Update".

I fell in love with the spotlight at age thirteen when I played a gangster's dumb blonde girlfriend in my middle school musical. I had an awakening on stage that opening night when a crowd of hundreds of people laughed at something I said. I found a new sense of self when being *funny*. Maybe it's the intense external validation, but I feel most myself when being silly and ridiculous. I feel free and uninhibited.

In seventh grade, I was cast as the lead in *Mulan*. Yeah, I know. It's super inappropriate for a predominantly white, Catholic school to pick *Mulan* for their musical, but alas, there I was in Imperial, being Mulan. This wasn't necessarily a funny role, but I absolutely loved acting and singing and diving into character. The only thing I didn't like is I had to be the *same* character every time and memorize lines. I also decided after that musical I would rather play the funny side character than the main character.

Well, I guess I would rather be the funny main character: the best of both worlds.

In my freshman year of high school, my mom asked me if I wanted to go to an improv class.

"What's *that*?" I asked her.

"My friend at work does it," she started. She was sitting in our basement at her desk, studying for her Nurse Practitioner degree. "It's like theater but you just make up funny stuff. There's no script." *Woah*, I thought. *It's like it was made for me.* My interest was piqued. "I think it's mostly older people like my age but I think you'd be fine. There's a class that starts on Sunday. Do you want me to take you this weekend?" My mom asked.

I remember standing in front of her desk and feeling at a crossroads. I could say no and just move on with my regular activities exclusive to high school and stay in my comfort zone, or I could go and make stuff up and try to be funny with a bunch of forty-year-olds whom I had never met. And I thought, *well Tina Fey didn't get anywhere by saying no to things.*

"Yes," I heard myself say. There it was: the first of many *yes, and*s.

A few days later, I found myself standing outside of a boarded up concrete building with no sign that said, "Improv Class This Way." My mom and I stood on the sidewalk and stared at the boarded-up doors and windows. Then we heard loud screams and shouts from inside. My eyes widened and I froze.

"Maybe this wasn't a good idea," I said nervously to my mom, inching back toward the minivan.

"No, it's fine. Knock on this," she said, and walked up toward a larger piece of plywood blocking an opening. I walked up and knocked. The shouts had turned into what sounded like ritual chanting. My heart was racing. And then–

"*Hello!*" The makeshift door swung open and a tiny lady with a pixie cut popped her head out aggressively, her tiny fingers gripping the edge of the plywood to conceal the inside. "Are you here for improv?" she asked excitedly, with a dimply smile.

"Uhm, yeah," I tried to sound confident, but I was a little freaked out. The noises coming from inside had evolved into animal mating calls.

SWOOSH! The pixie lady swung the plywood door wide open and stretched out her hand to welcome me inside. "Come on in!" She cheered. She had gift wrapping ribbon tied into her short blonde bob.

I stepped into the building and was instantly freaked out. It was a completely dilapidated old sandwich shop with rafters hanging from the ceiling and half-torn-out floorboards on the ground. It was cold, drafty, and kind of foggy from all the dust floating in the air. I looked to my left and saw a tiny wooden stage with seven adults dancing around in a circle and making weird noises. In the back of the room were eight black chairs in a circle. I looked back up at the pixie lady who was smiling wide, ear to ear. I had that tingly adrenaline feeling in my chest and arms. I couldn't tell if it was good or bad.

"Alright, I'll be back in two hours," my mom said and walked right out of the door. *Wait, but—*

I stared at the pixie lady with doe eyes and a forced smile.

"I'm Penelope!" she reached her hand out forcefully to shake mine. "I'm the level zero coach! I'll be teaching your class. This one right here is level three. They're just finishing up!" I watched the seven adults come down off the little stage and go sit down in the circle of chairs. They started talking about what it felt like to dance and scream in a circle. I stood and watched for a few minutes, and they all got up, told each other good job, and walked out past me, nodding and smiling.

They were like *real life* hipsters who I had seen on Tumblr. They had beards and tortoise shell round glasses and skinny jeans and flannels and tattoos and red lipstick and blue hair. They were *so cool*. They were like people from *movies*.

The other people from level zero started showing up behind me. They were all middle aged, white men. I looked at them awkwardly, wondering what my mom had gotten me into.

"Hi, I'm Kelly," I waved to a few guys. The only other times I was hanging out with middle aged men were when I was talking to my uncles at Christmas parties. It was a strange dynamic for my fifteen-year-old self. By the time everyone showed up, I realized I was the only girl in the class, and the youngest *by far*.

I was so uncomfortable, but I reminded myself again famous people like Tina Fey didn't get to where they are by being too comfortable and shy. I pushed through the nervous, tingly feelings and forced a smile and an open mind. Luckily, I had Penelope, so I felt kind of safe and tried to relax and have a good time. After all, this improv thing sounded really fun. *And* my mom was already gone, so I figured if I was stuck there for two hours, I might as well make the most of it. And I did.

We started playing games. Things like Zip, Zap, Zop and Pass That Sound, which are classic improv games I don't know how to explain very well. We made weird noises and silly body poses and walked around pretending to be ridiculous characters. It was so silly! It was so fun! And I kind of loved watching grown men be silly and play make believe—they were like kids! You are never too old to play make believe; I'll stand by that until I die.

It was also on that first day I learned the famous First Rule of Improv: yes, and. I fell in love with this famous rule. It has become my life's mantra—so much so, I tattooed it on my arm. It's really tiny, but it stays with me as a reminder to take life one step at a time. If only High School Kelly knew College Kelly would one day get a tattoo! Life is silly like that.

"Yes, and" is the first rule of improv because without it, you can't do much. "Yes, and" means you accept whatever your partner says as the truth. You shouldn't ever deny what your partner says. For example, if I start a scene running in yelling, "Doctor! Doctor! Help! My arm is falling off!" and my partner replies, "No, it's not! And I'm not your doctor—I'm your weird neighbor!"

Well, our scene dies and it's awkward. So the "yes, and" approach is to help keep things moving because it's hard to make shit up on the spot.

If I start the scene with, "Doctor! Doctor! Help! My arm is falling off!" and my partner responds, "**Yes, and** you're pregnant! What a predicament!" We can move forward and keep doing whatever weird scene the two of us will make up and by the end, we'll have wound up somewhere completely unexpected.

What I love about the "yes, and" rule is it forces scene partners to listen to one another, instead of having their own precious agendas. If someone starts a scene by calling you the doctor, but you were planning on being the weird neighbor, well too bad! You're the doctor now. You have to adapt! It's a team effort, and you build the scene together. Do you see how that works?

You don't have to plan out the whole scene in your head and try to get your partner on board. No! The "yes, and" method allows you to build a world together, one step at a time. If done well, you're able to organically build a unique world together neither of you could have thought up on your own. Every single scene winds up in some magically unexpected place—and that's the beauty of improv.

Two hours of laughing and acting out scenes went by quickly, and before I knew it, I was saying goodbye to Greg and Doug.

"See you next week!" I smiled and waved. I absolutely loved it. My mom pulled up in the minivan. I said bye to Penelope and hopped in the car, giddy to tell my mom about all the fun games we played.

The place is called The Improv Shop, and they had just bought that new location and were renovating it to be a comedy club and teaching center. The founders hailed from Chicago, the Improv Capitol, and were previous teachers and performers at renown improv theaters like Second City, Improv Olympic, and Upright Citizen's Brigade.

I took improv classes at The Improv Shop all four years of high school. Before I could drive, my parents would drop me off in the minivan every Saturday.

"Can you just park around the corner?" I'd ask nervously. "I don't want them to see my parents dropping me off." I was embarrassed. It wasn't like cheer practice. These were adults, and I wanted to fit in. I must have done a good job too! One day, I walked out of practice with friends from class, and my mom walked up to us on the sidewalk.

"Hey, Kell, how was it?" she asked.

"Great! This is Mark and Stephanie!" I gestured toward my forty-two-year-old friends. I had totally forgotten about not wanting people to know my age.

"Wait!" Stephanie gasped. "You're Kelly's *mom!* Wait, Kelly! How old are you?" Her head was whipping back and forth between me and my mom.

"I'm fifteen!" I giggled.

"Oh my God," Stephanie breathed out, clutching her chest. "I am so sorry," she walked up to my mom. "We had no idea! We thought she was like in her twenties or something! MAN! We have made some really inappropriate jokes, if we would have known—"

"Oh no!" My mom swatted her hand down. "Kelly's heard it all before. I'm the one that told her to sign up!"

Getting to act out crazy scenes with fun-loving people was the best two hours of my week. I looked forward to it every Saturday morning. On my sixteenth birthday, I walked into practice and my teammates surprised me with a giant pretzel in the shape of a sixteen. They sang me happy birthday, and after practice we all went out to lunch to celebrate. Meanwhile, I could hardly bring myself to text my high school friends and organize a party that would be good enough for them. I usually opted out of doing anything for my birthday. But the improv community made my Sweet Sixteen extra special.

By my senior year, I was on an actual team. By then, The Improv Shop had bought a second location with two stages and a bar! The community was growing exponentially, and I was proud to have something like this in St. Louis. Turns out, you don't have to be from New York or Los Angeles to be cool, important, and funny.

Being on a team meant I practiced with my own group and we got to perform shows *on the stage*! My team was called Shenandoah, named after the street we practiced on, and we were an all-female long form group, meaning we did twenty-five-minute shows with one developing story plot. Short form improv is just playing a series of games similar to those on the show *Whose Line Is It Anyway?*

Our ages ranged from seventeen to sixty, and to this day, I am forever grateful for this unique female friend group I got to be a part of. If we didn't perform at The Improv Shop, we would perform at local bars around St. Louis. Sometimes I would come into school the next day with black X's on my hands from marking me as under twenty-one at the bar.

"What are those?" the girls at the infamous lunch table would ask. I never knew what to say. The Improv Shop was like my secret life outside of high school. It was my escape on the weekends! I had an entirely separate friend group that consisted of twenty, thirty, forty, fifty, and sixty-year-olds—who were all really funny and who I got along with!

When I went to college, I auditioned for the short form improv team called K.A.R.L. I thought I was a shoo-in, a natural, an obvious pick! I had so much experience in such a niche thing! But I didn't make it. I was surprised and humbled, and it only made me want to join more. I loved the people I had met in auditions, and I would see them hanging out on campus and wish to be included. I tried out again in my spring semester of freshman year, and I made it.

Don't ask what K.A.R.L. stands for; it's a very exclusive secret. K.A.R.L. is a group of wildly intelligent, ferociously spirited, and astronomically gifted people. There are usually about ten to fifteen of us, depending on the semester. We practice three times a week, two hours each. It's a lot, isn't it? We probably don't need to practice that much, but it's just so much freaking fun. Six hours a week of watching your friends be insane and doubling over and crying of laughter is time well-fucking-spent. It's organized chaos disguised as an extracurricular activity.

Our shows at WashU are very well-attended and, I would argue, a staple of the WashU experience. We perform three times a semester, and our shows usually attract around three hundred people—which is insane to me. People come to the show before going out and sneak in beer and wine to pregame while watching us make fools of ourselves in front of a lecture hall. Our shows are without a doubt my best memories from college. Everyone who I've had the chance to be on K.A.R.L. with will be invited to my wedding. If you're on K.A.R.L. and reading this, this is your official invite to my wedding. Date: TBD.

As I write this, we are still amidst the Covid-19 pandemic, and I'm unsure if I will be able to perform with K.A.R.L. again, as I am a senior. I'm also the captain this year, so it's been difficult to lead the group during these uncertain times. I'm hoping I get one last chance to shine on stage with my best friends, but it's looking like that won't happen. The good news is: K.A.R.L. is a family of past and present members who keep in touch from near and far, and I have no doubt that K.A.R.L. will continue to be a part of my life post-graduation, which is perhaps the greatest gift college has given me (besides a kick ass diploma, obviously).

After shows, we host parties, and these parties are the liveliest, goofiest parties I have ever attended. Imagine a small group setting with drinking games and the funniest people on campus: things get silly. There are two other improv teams at school, and we all support one another by going to each other's shows and after-parties. Improv parties always, and I mean *always*, end unexpectedly and in weird places you would have never guessed, but they're hilarious nonetheless—much like a scene.

Improv is the silliest, most ridiculous thing in the world. I don't know if I'm very "good" at it, but I love it so much I don't even care.

Life is like improv. We're all just making shit up and rolling with the punches, right? Hoping every now and then we laugh? Life is a series of "yes, ands"; a series of listening to the universe, God, or pure chance and making little decisions as we go. We might have our own idea of how we want our lives to go, but it's not a one-man show.

We can try to plan out our lives in our heads, and we might think we know what's best (or what's funniest). But the truth is, we can't do that and we probably aren't as funny as we think we are.

Living by the "yes, and" mantra means trusting whatever happens will lead to something miraculous we couldn't have conjured up in our heads. This means saying yes to uncomfortable things when presented with an opportunity. This means adapting quickly when things change. This means listening to friends, family, and significant others in conversation and responding one step at a time, making sure to listen to what they have to say before you craft a response in your head. This means letting go of control and learning how to roll with the punches.

This means putting yourself out there, taking risks, and trusting even if shit hits the fan, at least it will be funny.

Golden Ticket

———

My dad graduated high school and started painting houses, working at a grocery store, and washing dishes in a pizza shop. His parents didn't go to college. His two older siblings didn't go to college. His neighbors didn't go to college. Nobody went to college. It wasn't in anyone's mind as an option. It was a foreign concept–a fleeting word with little meaning.

My dad relives his college story at least once a month, and it just about brings him to tears every time. My younger brother and I have grown up with his college story as the backbone and the mantra of our upbringing. We view education as the golden ticket in this family, and we don't take it lightly.

My dad was twenty-one when he met a pilot at a family party. He asked the pilot question after question about how he became a pilot. He answered he went to Parks College in Cahokia, Illinois. One random day while painting, my dad dropped his paint roller and got in his car and started driving. My dad drove around for hours, searching for Parks College in Cahokia, Illinois.

He finally found it and walked right up to the main office, still wearing his cut off jean shorts covered in paint. He walked in through the doors and up to a reception desk.

"Can I help you?" A woman asked.

"Yeah," my dad huffed, "I want to go here." The woman laughed.

"It's April. It's the middle of the semester. Come back for registration in August." My dad left and drove back to Cahokia months later for registration. He walked right back through those same doors and was told he needed at least Calculus I to enroll in the aeronautical engineering program. He had graduated high school with geometry and never even took basic algebra.

He went to Forest Park Community College for two and a half years just taking math classes, while maintaining his three other jobs. His parents thought he was crazy for wanting to go to college. It was just a massive expense and a waste of time.

After two and half years, my dad finally enrolled in St. Louis University's Parks College of Engineering. He paid his entire tuition by keeping his jobs and taking out several Pell Grants. He finally paid them off when he was forty-five, and my mom threw him a huge party.

He drove an hour to campus every day. His classes were an every-day-eight-to-five. He worked overnight at the grocery store. He failed his classes. It was hard. He had no friends. He hardly had any food. He ate the expired food they threw out at the grocery store. He locked himself in the library and hunched his head over his textbook, desperately trying to make sense of the high-level math that just didn't come naturally to him.

The other guys in his classes were in fraternities and had answers to all of the homework and the tests passed down from their brothers, so they were doing very well. But my dad didn't know them, or anyone, and didn't have time to *get* to know them because he was working three other jobs to pay his tuition.

But he kept going. He didn't have a choice. His other option was to drop out and go right back to his house in Florissant and paint houses and work at the grocery store for the rest of his life. Going to school to be an engineer was his ticket out. Sure, he *liked* airplanes, but he also wanted to secure a financially stable future for himself, and he saw engineering as the answer.

After three years of intense, grueling work, he graduated second in his class and was the only one offered a job at Boeing. The hard, honest work paid off. It's a miracle, really. My dad is the most creative, artistic, and imaginative person I know. I'm just like him, and studying engineering would probably give me a stroke. So the fact he did it, against the grain of his brain-wiring, is much more impressive.

After working for Boeing as an aeronautical engineer for several years, meeting my mom, and moving to Seattle, he decided he didn't want to work for anybody else. He quit his job, moved back to St. Louis, and lived with my mom's parents—in their basement—for two years while he started his own business, Brevé Coffee, which he still runs today.

He could have stayed at Boeing forever, and I imagine we'd have a lot more money or something. But my dad's independence can't be bought. It's not about the coffee, it's about owning his own business and doing whatever the hell he wants every day and knowing he's earned it.

"Do you have any regrets, Dad?" I asked him recently in the car. It was January 2021, and we were driving back from Rolla, Missouri where we had just trained a café owner how to run his new coffee shop.

"None."

My mom helped my dad start the coffee business and ran it with him for fifteen years. When I was in sixth grade, she realized she was dead set on sending my brother and I to Catholic high schools, so she went back to work as a nurse to help pay for it. But as Ryan and I got older, it became clear nursing and the coffee business wouldn't be enough to put us through college.

In 2012, my mom drained what little money had been saved for Ryan and me to go to college, took a second mortgage out on the house, and enrolled in St. Louis University's Nurse Practitioner program. She was forty and still working work full time. Three years later, she graduated from SLU and accepted a job at WashU as a Nurse Practitioner in Hematology.

This was her plan all along: to work at WashU. WashU employees receive a tuition benefit, meaning their children can attend Washington University in St. Louis for *free*. If they can get in, that is.

"What even *is* WashU? I've never heard of that," I scoffed at my mom in the car. I was probably in middle school. "No way I'm staying in St. Louis. I'm outta here." Jeez. The irony drapes over me as I write this from Imperial, Missouri, a senior in college living at home with my parents.

"It's a world-class institution, Kelly! It's like one of the best schools in the country!" my mom shouted, trying to get through to me.

I wanted the traditional, Midwestern college experience: a SEC school with a football team, big-ass tailgates, ivory-clad sorority houses, a glamorous cheerleading team, and thousands of Instagram followers that loved to watch me drink out of a red solo cup every weekend.

"You're smart enough to get in," my mom sighed. "If you can just get in, it's *free*. Do you get that? I don't know if your dad and I can afford some big out-of-state school anyway! At least just look it up. The campus is beautiful."

Sure enough, I looked it up and my jaw dropped to the floor. It looks like fucking Hogwarts. *"This is in St. Louis?"*

"Yes! Go! *Please!*" My mom yelled back.

And we were silent as I began to contemplate a different path. *Why had I never seen this place?* The acceptance rate on Google read 15 percent. *Shit, I couldn't get in. Or could I?* My mom seemed to think I was smart enough to get in, so I started to believe maybe I could. I wasn't the smartest person in school by any means, but I had drive like nobody's business.

Once I started doing research on WashU, I discovered a new realm of "the college experience." I saw similar schools on Google like Northwestern, USC, Georgetown, Vanderbilt, NYU, Columbia, etc. They all had famous alumni like Seth Meyers, George Lucas, Obama, and Lady Gaga. *Are these where the cool and important people go?* I wondered. It didn't look like they partied or had big football teams, but a degree from a place like this was a badge of prestige for the rest of your life . . . and your future kids' lives too.

"Your mother and I didn't have anything close to an opportunity like this," my dad said to me. "You will go *so far* in life. You'll be so much more successful than us. . ." He trailed off. I could always sense some resentment or sadness in his voice, which is understandable. Parents always want their kids to have it better than they did, but *being the kid* makes me feel guilty sometimes, which is why I work so hard. It's like if I can work hard enough, I'll deserve it. So that's what I do, whether it's healthy or not.

It started to sink in what a massive opportunity free tuition at WashU was, and I shifted gears. I wanted it; *badly.* I locked in and focused. I got straight A's in high school, joined clubs, and did all of the things WikiHow recommends to get into a selective school. I barely did well enough on the ACT—without a tutor—to scrape together a super score with a fighting chance.

In my senior year of high school, I applied to WashU's Sam Fox School of Design and Visual Arts. I later found out my friends didn't think I would get in. Yes Man applied to the engineering school. WashU was his dream school too. If I'm being honest, that's probably a reason I let myself date him for so long. I figured if we went to the same college, we'd never have to break up—a logical plan!

I had been at an improv show with my team from The Improv Shop when acceptance emails came out.

"And that's our show, ladies and gentleman!" Nancy beamed. "Thank you for coming to see Shenandoah! Again, we are an all-female, long-form improv group! Our next show will be in January. Thanks for coming, everyone!"

I looked out into the tiny crowd of maybe twenty people and found my parents and Yes Man, clapping with forced smiles. It had been an awkward show. Sometimes improv is kind of weird and not that funny. It probably has something to do with the fact it's never planned out and there's no script.

I stepped off the six-inch platform we called a "stage" and walked toward my family. We hugged and made small talk with the other indie improv community members. We exited through the back alley, and the wet winter air stung our faces as we searched for our car with hunched shoulders. I slid in the backseat and Yes Man cozied up next to me from the other side. It was eleven already. I reached into my purse and pulled out my phone. I had a text message from Joe Bopp.

"I heard WashU Early Decisions came out. Have you heard anything?" The text read.

My stomach dropped. I shakily handed my phone to Yes Man so he could read my screen. His eyes widened. Since I applied Early Decision, I was finding out in December and he had to wait until March since he Applied Regular Decision. Applying Early Decision means if you are accepted, you have to attend. If you apply Regular Decision, you still have a choice after acceptance on whether to attend or not. If I got in, I was going.

"Um . . ." I stuttered toward my parents in the front seat. It was pitch black outside and the red and white lights from other cars were spinning through the windows. "I think ED decisions came out tonight."

"Well, did you get an email?" My mom asked matter-of-factly.

"Uh . . ." I opened my email on my phone. There it was. Washington University in St. Louis Office of Admissions. My finger tapped on the email and I held my breath and closed my eyes.

It was a link.

I let out a sigh.

"Okay, it's just a link to the admissions portal. I'll just . . . wait until I get home." We had another forty minutes in the car and we had to drop Yes Man off. He squeezed my shoulder and smiled at me. The suspense hung coldly in the air, shivering and tensing our bodies as if we were still outside. It was nearly silent the rest of the way home.

I walked into my house like it was haunted. Something scary and unknown waited upstairs for me and I wasn't sure if I wanted to know. This was it. Getting into WashU would alter the trajectory of my life. As would not getting in. I was either going to an elite, highly ranked, prestigious university or going to a state school on scholarship to join a sorority and a cheerleading team.

"Alright, Kelly!!" My dad cheered as I walked slowly upstairs to my room. I tried to mutter something back under my breath, but it didn't come out. I pulled out my phone and started recording myself. I like to document big moments like these.

I scrolled through Google photos recently to find it, and there it was on December 9, 2016: the before and after videos side by side. I had never watched them. I tapped on the first one.

I walk into my neon purple bedroom, and I look like a classic deer in the headlights. My eyes are hollow and my breathing is audibly shallow. I have fake eyelashes and long, painted nails.

"WashU . . ." I breathe out, "released their Early Decisions." My mouth is dry and I lick my lips and take another deep breath. "It's a week early. . . . Earlier than I expected." My eyes stare blankly at my back wall. "It's okay either way. . . ." My voice shakes airily. "Oh my god. I'm so nervous." Video ends.

December 9, 2016

Age 17, senior year of high school

I got in.

"I just got into WashU and *I can't wait to be rich and famous! Ah!*"

The next video erupts into a loud, singsong-y Kelly prancing around her room making dramatic facial expressions and opening her mouth as wide as it possibly goes and moving her tiny hands up and down frantically.

"Oh my gosh! *You don't understand!*" I stare into the camera and go silent. "I've been working *since the seventh grade* for this! Holy shit. . . . My life is going to explode. . . ." Again, my eyes dart across the room and go blank. The opportunity—the lifestyle I believe it warrants me—*the trajectory.* I got the life trajectory I worked for. I won the lottery. You can see it all sinking in. I come back to the camera and smile.

"I can't wait to work my ass off! My *offspring* are going to be wealthy and have a good life! I did it!" I sigh into the camera and my eyes roll into the back of my head. "Oh my god. . . . I did it." Another sigh.

I went downstairs, hugged my parents, and fell to the floor crying. It was emotional. I had flashbacks of my mom working full time and going back to school so she could get a WashU job, not for herself, but for me. All the hard work of my parents and I really did pay off, and it was an incredibly pivotal moment that changed my life. I was ready to not take a second of it for granted.

In March, Yes Man was also accepted into WashU. I fell to the floor again and cried when he called and told me. I was really dramatic, but it meant we wouldn't have to break up or do long-distance! I saw this as a chance for us to have a shot! For us to potentially get *married!* It didn't even cross my mind sometimes people grow up and grow apart. Nevertheless, I was ecstatic and eager to start a journey for myself and also with Yes Man.

No one from my high school had gone to WashU in recent years that I knew of. I remember telling my friends how excited I was at the lunch table one day.

"WashU doesn't like . . . tailgate and party, do they?" Irena asked, making a skeptical, disgusted look. *How could anyone go to a college that isn't a SEC state school with a football team*, she was probably thinking.

"No, I don't think so," I said, knowing very well I would be in the library on Saturday mornings while my friends from high school would be day drinking and having the time of their lives.

And I was right. I have spent most Saturday mornings in studio or in the library. Most times, I'm not even hungover because by the time Friday night rolls around, I am so tired from the week I am just grateful to go to bed early, knowing I can have a good night's sleep before I work all day Saturday. I've had my fair share of college nights drinking and dancing, but it's nothing like the movies. . . . And nothing like the state schools on my friends' Snapchat stories.

I knew it would be like this going in, but I was willing to sacrifice my Saturdays for the countless days my parents sacrificed to even place this opportunity in my lap.

What I didn't know was my entire life's bubble was about to burst. Every belief I was raised with would be challenged. Every value system I grew up with would be debased. I would meet people with far different perspectives than mine.

I would be confronted with difficult conversations about politics, mental health, sexuality, race, and religion, and I wouldn't know what to say. I would be called out and learn the deeper meanings of my words. I would be completely stretched inside out, broken, put back together, and transformed into what I am today.

Stretched Inside Out

<hr />

I sat on the floor of my dorm room and looked at myself in the mirror that hung on my closet door. I let out a defeated sigh. I didn't want to do it, but I knew I had to. High School Kelly had to go.

I dug my fingers into a jar of coconut oil and scraped out white chunks with my long, glossy pink nails. I rubbed the chunks between my fingers as they turned into oil. I closed my eyes and took a deep breath. My oily fingers reached up to my eyelids and started rubbing and pulling out my fake eyelashes.

It only took a week at WashU to realize the show was over. My nails were so long and perfect that I wasn't getting my hands dirty in my drawing and 3D design studios. I didn't have forty-five minutes to spare on a drive to have my stupid fake eyelashes refilled. I didn't have ten minutes to rub orange lotion all over my body and pretend to be tan. I didn't have the budget anymore for these extraneous things.

I went into the bathroom and rubbed my fingers with acetone and clipped my nails to stubs. I got in the shower and scrubbed my body as hard as I could until there was no fake tanner left. I stepped out of the shower and looked into the foggy mirror. I was pale with dark circles under my lash-less eyes. I put my hair in a ponytail and walked down to the studio, ready to get my hands dirty.

"Wow, you use *so* much makeup," a girl had said to me as we were getting ready for a party. I paused and felt a wave of insecurity. *So too much makeup is bad*, I noted. I so desperately wanted to fit in. I so desperately wanted to appear like I was smart enough and deserved to be there. Apparently *smart* and *too much makeup* didn't go together (which is bullshit, by the way).

My idea of *college girls* was everyone had long, blonde hair, wore over-sized t-shirts, and had perfectly tanned long legs with a bubbly personality to match. The girls in Sam Fox wore high waisted pants, or corduroy, leather, cropped, cashmere, neon, ripped, or recycled denim, with chopped black hair, winged eyeliner, and a septum piercing to match. I had no idea what to wear. As someone who normally copied off of others to fit in, I suddenly had no one to copy off of. Everyone in art school had a signature look.

WashU has a notorious reputation for being one of the least socioeconomically diverse universities in the country. If I thought going to high school with kids who owned luxury SUVs was a lot, now I was running with kids whose parents owned the manufacturing plants for those SUVs.

"Your high school was like a Kate Spade purse." A friend of mine observed one time. "My high school was like a Prada or Gucci bag." If kids from my high school vacationed in Florida, these kids vacationed in Greece. If kids from my high school had Swarovski bracelets, these kids had solid gold Cartier ones. If my dad owned a small coffee business, these kids' parents might as well have invented coffee itself.

WashU might be in St. Louis, but it's in a different dimension.

I point this out only to give you a clearer picture of the student body and to back up my point I go to college with a shit ton of rich kids, which is fine except for when they want to go out to dinner every weekend or don't know what I'm talking about when I'm stressing about my student loans, which I took out just to cover room and board. It's kind of frustrating.

During my first week on campus, I heard other freshman complaining about how they didn't get into Harvard and UPenn, and how their friends thought they were stupid for going to WashU. I worked so hard just to get in by the skin of my teeth. I felt inferior and a little pissed off. How could some people not see the immense privilege just standing on our campus was? To even have a school like WashU on your list of options—and to go to college in the first place—is an incredible feat. I felt like I was in a different universe.

Most of the kids I've met in college have been from New York City, somewhere in New Jersey, Los Angeles, Chicago, DC, or somewhere on the East Coast. If you know anything about these cities, it's they tend to be very progressive and Missouri is, well, *not*.

When I arrived at WashU my freshman year, I experienced a true culture shock I could not have anticipated.

Though I knew WashU attracted students from all over the world, I was deeply unaware of how my experiences of going to small, Catholic schools in Missouri for twelve years would affect my transition into college. For those twelve years, I believed everyone in the world was also white, Catholic, and upper-middle class. A massive culture shock was necessary.

I went from living in a tiny bubble in Imperial, Missouri, thinking everyone in the world looked like me, acted like me, prayed like me, and believed in the same things as me, to being thrown into an environment where it seemed like everyone was on the same page *except* for me.

I nearly had a heart attack the first time I went to do laundry freshman year. I opened the door and my eyes landed on a plastic box on the wall that was filled with plastic wrapped squares. A sticker on the box read, "practice safe sex!"

Ah! What the fuck? I thought. I nearly dropped my laundry basket. *Were those condoms? Ew! Why would a university encourage kids to have sex?* We weren't allowed to drink, but *here's free condoms for everyone! Knock yourself out! Really?*

My sex education went something like this:

"Kelly," my mom started after turning off the TV in the middle of an unexpected sex scene from *Pretty Little Liars*. "TV is not real life. TV is written by the devil, and people in real life don't just go around and have sex with strangers. You can have sex all you want, but you will get an STD, die, get pregnant, and go to Hell. So that's up to you." I still question the chronological order of that sequence of events, but nevertheless, I believed her.

All they told us in Catholic school was *not to do it.* They didn't really say what "it" was, just not to do it unless you're trying to have a baby and are already married. For all I knew in middle school, sex was just hugging naked under the covers. I had never heard the words safe and sex in the same sentence before.

I told my friend Sanjana about this one night when we were doing homework together. Honestly, I thought it was very funny only a few months later.

"Kelly, that's seriously so fucked up," she said, her face turning very serious. "You weren't taught how to physically express yourself. That's so unfair!" And all of a sudden, I felt defensive.

"Well, I mean . . ." I started thinking out loud, "That's how I grew up, that's my religion and what my family believes in, so I don't know if it's *fucked up.* It's just different." And then I started wondering what it means to physically express yourself. I wondered if I was missing out. I wondered who had taught her how to express herself. What does that even mean?

Should my mom have told me it was a normal human sensation to feel aroused? I don't know. Should she have tossed me a vibrator at age fifteen and said *knock yourself out*? Probably not? But maybe?

I was going to the bathroom one day in a stall at the art school. This was a few weeks after the condoms in the laundry room incident. A poster of a nude girl shown from neck to knee, painted like she was also going to the bathroom, was hanging on the stall door. The poster read, "X-Mag: WashU's New Sex-Positive Magazine".

My jaw dropped, and I blushed. I kept reading it. *Sex-positive?* I thought. *How can a university allow students to talk about sex so openly? Is this allowed?* I grappled with these questions in my mind, bewildered. I remembered all of the times in elementary and high school when a special guest had come to our religion class to give us a sex talk that was really just a Jesus talk. I remembered my mom screaming at me while I watched TV, making me turn off any show that so much as showed people making out. *Were WashU Health Services and X-Mag the devil, just like the people that write TV shows?* I sat in that bathroom stall for twenty minutes having this discussion with myself.

It was like everyone at WashU knew something I didn't. My friends, classmates, and even my professors' beliefs were projected as correct and obvious, the same way mine had been growing up in my surroundings. But now I was completely out of my context and suddenly, the things I grew up believing to be true were completely turned upside down. I started questioning *everything*.

I began to resent the bubble I grew up in. I was frustrated because I was starting to realize how ignorant I was and I blamed it on where I grew up. Because when you grow up in a world where everyone looks and thinks the same, you're never presented with other options, other beliefs, and other sides of the story. You're never challenged to think about *why* you think the things you do. You just *do* because everyone does, and everyone agrees and reinforces the idea you're right. It's an echo chamber.

October 18, 2018

Age 19, sophomore year of college

*My parents are educated, hardworking, God-loving peo-
ple. But are they wrong? Are my college friends right?
Do they have smarter and better parents than I do? Is
it because their parents went to Ivy League schools and
mine didn't? Is it because these people have more money
than I do and so they have better access to education, and
therefore are "correct" and more informed about these
things? Maybe. If I didn't already resent Imperial, Missouri
enough, now I do even more.*

The irony here is WashU is its own echo chamber. I
was taken out of my bubble and plopped into a different
bubble—a bubble where kids wear Canada Goose coats
in forty-degree weather, vacation in Europe during the
summers, have CEO fathers, a penthouse on the Upper
East Side, and think socialism is a really good idea if we
could just get it right. This is a joke, obviously. Not everyone is like this. And maybe socialism is a good idea, what
do I know? *Clearly not enough*, they would say.

Serendipitously, my four years of college coincided
with the four years of the Trump presidency. Every
possible issue ever was top-of-mind and relevant, and
rightfully so. Tension hung in the air over the campus.
Or maybe I'm the only one who felt it because I seemed
to walk on eggshells every day, scared I would say something wrong, and I did. Several times. But it's those
moments that have shocked me into realizing just how

big the world is and just how important it is to be open-minded and empathetic.

I could have been "cancelled" several times, especially during my freshman and sophomore years. Political correctness was a new language for me, and it took time to learn, along with a few mistakes. I'm still learning every day. There are just some things you don't know until you experience it, or listen to someone who actually has experience. That's the problem with living in a bubble: your exposure is limited. This goes for both ends of the spectrum.

In the beginning of my sophomore year, I voted for the first time. It was a Missouri State Senate Election. As I was walking to the polling station on campus, a friend of mine came up to me and gave me a hug.

"Kelly! Your first time voting! Aren't you excited that you get to vote for a woman on your first ballot?" she beamed with pride. She was wearing a foam Statue of Liberty hat and American flag patterned shorts. I noticed myself get uncomfortable. I had to think about why for a moment.

She had assumed who I was going to vote for, and that didn't sit well with me. To be honest, I was very torn between the two candidates at the time. My parents were sending me multiple text messages about who to vote for, which was really annoying, and my friends were talking about how bad that candidate was and how anyone with a brain would vote otherwise. I didn't know what I believed for myself. It was the first time I was in an environment where the opinions were different than ones I had heard before, and I wasn't expecting to have to really think about where I stood on these issues.

"Well, um, actually," I stuttered as my heart started to race, "I'm not totally sure that I'm going to vote for her." My friend stopped in her tracks and her smile vanished. She looked like she had seen a ghost.

"Wait . . . can you explain why you wouldn't?" she asked, visibly stunned.

"Well, my mom told me that since the last tax cut, she gets five hundred dollars a month more on her paycheck and all of that goes toward my room and board, which I'm already taking out loans for. So she wants me to vote to keep the tax plan," I said. That was my only reason. I didn't know anything about either of the candidates.

Her facial expression didn't change. She walked away abruptly, and I felt really uncomfortable for having to defend myself. At the time, I was very uneducated about Missouri politics and the effects of certain policies. I still am, if I'm being honest. It's very difficult to understand. But I've since learned it's important to be an informed citizen before you vote instead of just doing what your parents text you to do (and parents probably shouldn't text their kids that stuff).

One night during my sophomore year, I was at a party and somehow got on the topic of growing up in a place of violence. I started talking with my friend Amir about being afraid to ever go to Downtown St. Louis because every time I turned on the news, I heard about a shooting (which is another issue in and of itself). He listened so intently as I divulged the *hardships* of living only *forty minutes away* from a *dangerous city*. I felt like

I was shedding light on an issue he hadn't thought about because he isn't from here. He nodded slowly, and when I was finished, he took a deep breath and leaned back in his chair.

"Yeah." He sighed. "It's really rough to grow up like that," he kindly acknowledged. "It reminds me of being scared back home whenever our neighborhood got bombed."

That moment, to this day, is one of my most embarrassing moments. It takes a humble and patient friend like Amir to politely make you realize you said something ignorant. I don't even think his intention was to call me out—but I realized instantly I was out of place. His kindness and nonchalance in that moment stung worse than if I had been explicitly called out and been labeled as problematic. It made me confront just how small my bubble had been before WashU.

In the spring of my sophomore year, I opened a Snapchat from a group chat I was in. It was a photo of a stack of Pro-Life posters in my friend's hands. The caption read something like, "Just tore down all of these Pro-Life posters from the dining hall! Haha!" Everyone responded with "LOL" and "bahaha fuck yes!"

I saw it in the library and was so overwhelmed I started to cry a little bit. This has nothing to do with abortion. I'm Pro-Choice without a doubt. But the fact it was okay for someone at my school to go around and physically tear down posters for a cause they didn't believe in felt outrageously hypocritical to me. I didn't tear down the sex positive posters when they scared me and went against my beliefs. (Granted, this much more sensitive subject). But why could other people do this and be met with "haha yes!"?

I did not handle this situation well. This too, is another one of my most embarrassing moments. Later that night, I was hanging out with those friends and they asked how I was.

"Well, I'm actually really pissed off about that Snapchat today! It's so hypocritical to just go around and tear shit down that you don't agree with!" I started to cry, and I got up and stormed out of the room before anyone could respond to my outburst. I was morbidly embarrassed. I heard things every day I didn't agree with, and it took so much energy to keep my mind open and my mouth shut. I was willing to shift my perspective and change my opinions, every single day. It didn't feel like others were challenged the same way I was, perhaps because they were already on the "right" side of things. My mistake here was I ran away. Midterms stress, emotional turmoil with Yes Man, and this cherry on top caused me to lose my cool and make a scene.

I later met up with my friend who had sent the picture. I was in tears the whole time, trying to explain I had friends who go to the Pro-Life march in DC every year and they are good people. To me, it's not right to tear down causes that are other peoples' right to believe in.

It felt like I was being told religious people were dumb and deserved to be laughed at. It felt like an attack on how I grew up. I was frustrated everyone else thought what she did was okay. It felt like everything I was raised to believe was wrong in everyone else's eyes, and that was an emotional experience. Because if it was true everything I had grown up hearing was dumb, then was I dumb too? Were my family, friends, and some of my own beliefs really that worthless they deserved to be torn down and met with a "bahaha fuck yes"?

"Well," she started to defend herself, "as someone whose best friend had an abortion. . . ." She choked up, "I thought that it might be triggering for someone like her to see those posters, and I didn't want anyone to feel what my friend feels when she sees those things. I'm sorry if that upset you."

And just like that, all of my qualms and frustrations disappeared. A wave of compassion crashed into me, washing away my previous aggravations. I felt awful for making this situation about me and a big enough deal she had to disclose that information to me. I still think we shouldn't tear down others' beliefs, but there's a greater lesson here. This conversation taught me the importance of holding space for peoples' backgrounds, whether I know them or not. We don't always know what experiences people are harboring, and we may *never* know, but we can always hold empathy in our minds for the things we cannot see.

One summer, I took my friend Sage to a bar at the Lake of the Ozarks. The Lake is, well, more sheltered than Imperial, the opposite of WashU, and the furthest place from progressive. We walked in and I could tell she was uncomfortable.

"What's up?" I asked, checking in on her.

"Well," she laughed uncomfortably. "I'm definitely the only Asian person here. Hope nobody hates me!" She tried to play it off, but I could see she was tense. I hadn't considered she might feel out of place there.

"Sage! Relax." I tried to calm her down, "Nobody here is even thinking about that, and nobody hates Asians here, that's ridiculous. You're fine!"

I thought I was being calming and reassuring, but after a later conversation with Sage, she kindly explained to me I had denied her experience of feeling anxious by assuming nobody had a negative bias toward her as a person of color.

"You don't know what those people are thinking. It's a defense mechanism to assume they have no prejudice against people of color. You're standing up for them and invalidating the reasons I felt uncomfortable." Her voice was calm. She wasn't angry at all.

Why had I said that? Why would I defend a group of strangers, whose beliefs I am totally unaware of, but disregard Sage's feelings, while fully aware of the racist remarks she's encountered throughout her life? Well, I didn't want to believe the people I've grown up around were racist. Selfishly, I didn't want to confront a difficult conversation. But Sage wasn't asking me to uncover those answers or even defend her. She just wanted me to understand how she had felt in that moment.

It wasn't her responsibility to educate me. She could have never said anything and just never spoke to me again, writing me off as someone who would never get it. She was courageous and vulnerable enough to even mention she was uncomfortable. She took the time to help me understand when we walk into rooms together, specifically white spaces, there is an extra layer of anxiety she confronts that I don't. She wasn't asking me to do anything about it, she just wanted me to understand and be mindful of it.

I asked her what kind of response would have made her feel better.

"Just listen," she said simply. "Just listen to people and accept their experience as their truth."

It's through these sometimes-uncomfortable discussions I've learned the most about the world. The reality is everyone has their own lens through which they see the world, their own nuanced upbringing, their own personal baggage. By taking the time to sit down and give people space to share their experiences, and *accepting them as truth*, I've learned *so much* about multifaceted topics I wouldn't have otherwise engaged with.

The culture shock I experienced was a blessing. Imagine living in an environment where everyone is the same as you for your entire life and never questioning anything! There's a lot I would have missed out on had I not gotten to be a part of this community. From race and religion to sex and politics, I've confronted, questioned, challenged, and embraced what presented itself to me to the best of my conscious ability.

Though I have still never been to a tailgate, and don't feel I've gotten in as much partying as I'd have liked for my "college experience," I am forever grateful for the endlessly fascinating, wildly inspiring, grossly overachieving peers I have been surrounded by. These people have pushed me to elevate my goals, believe I can achieve greater feats than I expected for myself, and taught me more about what it means to be a compassionate human being than any religion class could have.

WashU has challenged the absolute hell out of me personally, academically, politically, socially, and spiritually. I can't wait to graduate. I wouldn't be who I am if I hadn't been stretched completely inside out, broken, put back together, and pushed to a new limit of potential. I'm proud of who I've become.

And I'm looking forward to who I will be, because I'm only twenty-one and I have a lot left to learn.

Small Legs, Big Teeth

My social life at WashU was completely centered around Yes Man.

I created my social sphere with respect to him. I crafted a universe devoid of any reality in which he was not my boyfriend. In my head, we were the famous couple at WashU that had been dating for years. We were a dynamic duo. We were perfect for each other and everyone else loved watching us being in love. In my head, we were getting married on April 23, 2022 in WashU's Graham Chapel. In my head, we were practically already married.

It was all planned out. I had no doubt in my mind this would go according to plan, as things usually did for me.

Also in my plans was becoming famous. I wasn't sure what for—I'm still not—but it was going to be something big and fabulous with red carpets and my own Wikipedia page. Yes Man would be the perfect trophy husband. He was sweet, silent, and supportive. He was the rock and I was the balloon. He let me run the show, and whatever I said was final say.

"You'll come with me to New York, right?" I would say. "Because I'm going to have to go there with or without you and it would be nice to have you by my side.... Actually, I need you. I can't do any of this without you!" And I would hug him and thank him for being supportive and all the while, he had never even gotten a word in.

Sometimes I would ask him what his dreams and goals were. He would think about it, but I would start talking again. For someone who sure loves the "yes, and" idea, I wasn't listening very well, and it made for a lopsided scene where I was pushing my own ideas and making it all about me.

The irony is although I appeared to "wear the pants" in this relationship, I was desperately dependent on him. I loved the security our relationship gave me, especially once we had celebrated three years. I felt locked in. I noticed myself saying things to my friends about marrying him. It wasn't uncommon for people in Imperial, and St. Louis too, to get married right out of college.

I was used to seeing people get engaged on graduation day, married a year later, and have three kids and a white picket fence by the time they were twenty-six. I think this trend is on the decline now, but this is the narrative I grew up with, and this is how it was going to go down for me too.... In my head.

"Well, it'd be nice to just have that part of my life figured out so I can focus on my career and not worry about dating and shit." It was a box checked off of my list of things to do, and everything had been smooth sailing for three years so I figured, *this will do*. I guess it helped too our relationship was very real, and I loved him more than anything. I truly did.

Yes Man joined a fraternity and that meant, in my head, I had also joined the fraternity. I spent most of my weekends, when I wasn't trapped working in the studio, in their sweaty, sticky, beer-encrusted basement pretending to be entertained by boys throwing ping pong balls into cups. I became friends with his fraternity brothers and found myself determined to be a part, in some way, of their exclusive brotherhood.

I had joined a sorority, but we didn't have a house, and it was hard to connect with the girls during the one-hour meeting in a lecture hall once a week. I was searching for the type of friends like I had seen on TV, but this time it was more like *Friends* and *New Girl*. A coed friend group is what I was searching for.

I dragged my single friends to Yes Man's frat parties and nudged—well, more like shoved—them at other single guys and obnoxiously told them to flirt with each other. It wasn't long before my two closest friends at the time, Sophia and Rachel, were also dating boys in Yes Man's fraternity. Again, everything was going according to plan.

But I was envious of Yes Man's new brotherhood. Everyone seemed so close-knit. They were intensely conditioned to treat each other like brothers. My sorority was nothing like that. At first, I thought what they had was really special. Then—subconsciously, of course—I became threatened.

Yes Man was spending more time with them than me. He was reluctant to make concrete plans with me in an effort to keep his options open in case something like, perhaps, a beer pong tournament came up. When we were together, his eyes glazed over. Though this wasn't completely uncommon, I noticed a new air of indifference: complacency, or maybe even resentment. I could tell when he would lie in my bed with his eyes glued on the ceiling, he would have rather been somewhere else.

And what does an insecure girlfriend do when she feels threatened? I've learned she becomes clingy, possessive, and overbearing. And the more they behave this way, the further they push the disinterested boyfriend away. But of course, I didn't notice any of this! Because as I've also learned, the first stage of grieving loss is denial. I could feel him slipping away, and I couldn't accept that possibility because I needed a husband next to me on that red carpet—whenever it was going to be! I needed Yes Man because without Yes Man . . . who were my friends? Who was I going to marry? *Who was I?*

Yes Man's close friend at the time was a guy I will call Dance Man because one summer he turned down a software engineering internship in New York to go to a dance conservatory. He became a very good dancer that summer. One time, Dance Man and I even tried to start a podcast together. He is very creative and silly. When I met Dance Man my freshman year, he told me he had interned at NBC the summer before. I nearly spilled my drink.

"What?" My jaw dropped. "Like . . . *the* NBC? Like TV?" My heart stopped. He smiled, nonchalantly.

"Yeah! My mom used to be a producer at MTV. She has a friend from there that works at NBC now who helped me get it! I would be happy to connect you guys or just give you her email," he said, reaching for his phone in his back pocket.

I was stunned. This was the thing about WashU kids: they had connections, because they weren't from Imperial. They were from places where the *cool* and *important* people are. Places like New York and Los Angeles where you can be a producer at MTV.

And all of a sudden, my big crazy dreams received a dash of possibility. They seemed a little less crazy and a little, and I mean just a little, more tangible.

"*Oh my god, are you serious*?" I stepped toward him, my eyes bearing into his, completely drowning out the loud music and drunk girls spilling their drinks on me as they bumped passed me.

"Yeah, totally. She's super nice." He started texting me her email. "You know what, I'll just email you both tomorrow in a thread. She loves helping young people get jobs, and she'll love you."

A wave of memories of people preaching that, *it's all about who you know* became a real thing for me in that moment. Dance Man emailed myself and an HR manager at NBC the next day and off I went into a networking frenzy.

I updated my resume, I purchased LinkedIn premium, I joined the Entertainment Careers group through the career center at WashU, I reached out to local production studios in St. Louis and offered to start working for them, for free, immediately! Anything to get one sliver of relevant experience on my resume! I started emailing people way out of my circle—people in entertainment—asking them if they would be able to set up an informational phone call with me. I followed every single entertainment or media outlet on LinkedIn, saw if any WashU alumni worked there, and emailed every single one of them. WashU had seventy-six alumni who worked at NBC. You bet your ass I emailed every single one of them until LinkedIn notified me I had reached the out of network email limit for the month.

I went berserk.

If Dance Man could work at NBC, so could I, and I was going to do everything in my power to make sure I did. Oh! And the internships were in *New York City or Los Angeles*. There was a chance I would get to live in one of those cities *before I even graduated!* The opportunity was like a drug! Just the idea of an internship like that released a high level of dopamine that kept me vigilant, focused, and determined to get my foot in the door of the entertainment world.

March 4, 2019

Age 20, sophomore year of college

> *On Friday, March 15 at 3:00 pm, I'll have to enter the lobby at 50th West 50th Street, make a right, find Guest Reception, wait until I'm called, and then be given directions to the Late Night with Seth Meyers suite for an interview.*
>
> *Yes, at 30 Rockefeller Plaza.*
>
> *I'm making it happen, baby.*

I freaked out when the email from Lauren at Late Night with Seth Meyers popped up on my phone. I'll never forget it. I screamed and smiled so wide and tears welled up in my eyes and I called my parents, freaking out.

"You have to go!" My dad said. "Go to New York!" My dad has always pushed me to go after the things I want and has been more than supportive over the years.

The email said they could interview me over the phone. But the date of the interview happened to be over my spring break, and my family had racked up a ton of Southwest points, which meant I could fly for free.

I texted my friend Jonah, who was a senior on K.A.R.L. when I was a freshman and now lived in New York City. I asked if I could sleep on his couch for two nights. I believe he replied, "*YAAAAAASSSS.*" So that was taken care of. I was going to show up and walk into that building even if I never got the job. Just to be able to walk into 30 Rock and go up into the elevators would be a once in a lifetime opportunity.

I landed in New York on Thursday night. Every time I take the cab from LaGuardia into Manhattan feels like a movie, especially when I'm by myself and it's nighttime and all of the lights sparkle like magic. Jonah texted me and told me to meet him at a bar that was live streaming *RuPaul's Drag Race* and hosting drag performances on commercial breaks. *God, I love New York*, I thought.

The next day, I put on my fancy dress suit I wore at school for business presentations. I packed black high heels in my purse to change into when I arrived. Jonah was at work until seven that night. After the interview, I was going to meet up with some of Yes Man's friends who lived on the Upper East Side and were home for spring break.

I walked out of Jonah's apartment and onto the streets of New York City, by myself for the first time. And with a *very cool and important* place to go. I wasn't there on vacation. I was there on business. I started walking fast, eating up every second I got to blend in with the real New Yorkers. I hoped when people saw me, they would think I lived there too. I tried to not smile and make my face very serious, but it was hard. I was so giddy.

When I walked up to 30 Rock, my heart started racing at seeing all of the tourists out front with their selfie sticks. I politely brushed passed them and pushed through the revolving doors into the lobby. It was massively grandiose with a gold mural on the ceiling and sparkling black marble floors. There were bellmen dressed in suits and ties. I had to pee. I was also thirty minutes early. I mustered up the courage to walk up to a bellman.

"Hi, where's the restroom?" I asked. The bellman broke his poker face and looked down at me with a smile. I think the naivety was written all over my face.

"Downstairs and to the right, miss." His hand gracefully motioned toward a set of stairs.

"Thank you!" I turned around and walked with purpose down the stairs and wandered in circles until I found the bathroom. Once I did, I sat down and let out a big sigh. My armpits were so sweaty. I was nervous as hell. I reached down into my purse and pulled out my skinny black high heels, and switched out of my Adidas tennis shoes. I squeezed my feet into the heels and stood up, wobbly. It was going to be a long walk up.

I finally got directions from reception and headed to the elevator. There were dozens of rows of elevator banks, and each bank had twelve elevators. The elevators didn't have numbers on the inside or outside; there was a digital screen on the outside where you punched in the floor you needed. I messed up a few times, but I finally got into the right elevator. Some guys walked in behind me.

"I think we're gonna have to go back and redo that take," one guy said. *Ah! A take! TV lingo!* I screamed in my head. Just the thought of these guys filming something in this building that would later go on TV was crazy exciting to me.

I finally got to the floor where the *Late Night* office was. The ceilings were *so low* and made of white particle board stuff, and the carpet was old, grey, and musty smelling. There was nothing fancy about it. I was caught off guard. I wobbled over to glass doors that read *Late Night with Seth Meyers* and pulled, but they were locked. I stood, puzzled, for a moment before a girl saw me and opened it for me. I thanked her and she walked away briskly.

I walked into the office and immediately realized I was extremely overdressed. There were people running around all over in ripped jeans, flannels, and ponytails–nothing fancy about them. The office space was tiny too; I was shocked. I walked up to the reception desk, which was also tiny.

"Hi, I'm Kelly. I have a three o'clock with Lauren," I told the girl at reception. She looked only a little bit older than me.

"Okay, she'll be right out for you! Have a seat on the couch," she said. I sat down on the couch that was crammed right next to the makeshift-looking reception desk and realized everyone running around the office *was a young, white girl with brown hair. Just like me.*

Hmm, I thought. *Does every white girl from the suburbs have the same cliché dream? Small girl, big city?*

I completely botched the interview. I was nervous and sweaty and rambling. I hadn't even thought to prepare answers ahead of time because in that moment, I realized it was my *first* real job interview. I wanted it so badly I couldn't decide which stories to tell the HR girl so I talked quickly and excitedly.

"You're dressed awfully nice," she said while she was writing stuff down on a clipboard.

"Thank you," I said softly. My feet were dangling off the chair and I was sitting straight up on the edge of my seat.

"You're from St. Louis?" she asked, briefly looking up.

"Yes!"

"And you flew in for this?" It hit me real jobs *pay* for people to fly out for interviews. I immediately became conscious of how desperate I appeared.

"Well, I was going to be here for my spring break visiting family, so it worked out that I was able to stop by," I lied. I wished I had family to visit there. Little did she know my parents scraped together Southwest points for me to buy plane tickets and I was sleeping on a couch in a microscopic apartment.

"Oh, nice!" she smiled. "Okay, well I've got everything I need. Thank you so much for coming in, Kelly. You may or may not get an email from us in a month or so. Thanks!" She grabbed her clipboard and walked out of the room. I got up, shaking in my heels that I could hardly walk in, and made what felt like a walk of shame out of the office, acutely aware of how grossly overdressed I was as I felt my blazer stick to my sweaty back.

I went back down and found the same bathroom I went in before. I closed the stall door, sat down on the toilet, yanked the heels off, and pulled my Adidas back on. I changed into leggings and a t-shirt. I breathed out another sigh of relief. My armpits were still sweaty.

I walked outside, feeling free of all the nerves, but with a sinking feeling I had gotten the interview all wrong. Nevertheless, I was in New York City all by myself! I walked to Bryant Park and sat at a table. It was sunny and sixty, which was warm for March. I sat and just looked around for a while, romanticizing Future Kelly with a real job and a real apartment.

I took a cab to the Upper East Side and met Yes Man's friends outside of their apartment. I felt like a really cool girlfriend for being able to stop by and hang out with the boys without Yes Man being there. We sat around in a lounge room and talked about school. They asked how the interview went.

"So you're into all the comedy stuff then?" One guy asked.

"Yeah, I love it. It's so fun," I answered, trying to sound chill.

"Oh, that's right! You're on K.A.R.L.!" Another guy chimed in.

"Oh fuck!" A third guy piped up. "Last time I was there, Yes Man and I were still tripping so hard—it was *crazy*!"

He laughed and leaned back in his chair and took a hit from his juul.

Um.

Did he just say—?

I looked around and the table had gone silent and the guys' faces had turned pale. Their eyes darted back and forth between each other, avoiding mine.

"Fuck, dude," Guy 1 said to Guy 2. "She wasn't supposed to know about that. . . ." He put his head in his hands.

"Oh shit," said Guy 2 with the juul. "*Fuck!* I'm so sorry, Kelly. I'm such an idiot. He didn't want you to know."

My eyes froze, wide open. My arms and legs started to tingle. My heart felt like it was crawling up into my throat. My stomach started to boil. I started feeling dizzy as my heart pounded in my chest and I forced myself to stay calm. I was in front of his friends. I had to be chill. I had to appear unbothered.

"Oh." I forced a laugh. Actually, who am I kidding? I have no fucking clue what I said. I think I partially blacked out. It sucked. I was humiliated. I was the crazy girlfriend whose boyfriend told his friends to lie to me because if he didn't, it was assumed I would freak out. It wasn't even about the "recreational activities" he was apparently up to. It was the fact I was excluded and lied to about it. I was being kicked out the backdoor, and Yes Man was locking it behind me.

He needed space to figure himself out. He wanted to explore new people and *hobbies* apparently. That's what college is for. Looking back, I know I was suffocating him, especially with my half-jokes about getting married. But that being said, it would have been *really nice* to have Yes Man explain what he was feeling to me instead of dragging me around and slowly shutting me out, hoping I'd just leave on my own.

But that's Yes Man's thing. He can't say no. He can't say a lot of things. Yes Man's inability to express himself used to be endearing, but now it was a character flaw.

This wasn't the first time he had lied to me about something like this, and it wasn't the first time I had been humiliated in front of people and made out to look like the crazy girlfriend. The thing is, I probably wouldn't have cared about his new *hobbies* if I had been included or invited to partake. But the fact I was kept out of that world confirmed he thought I didn't belong, or he didn't want me to see him that way. Maybe he felt guilty. Maybe he was trying to see himself in a new world and explore who he was without me. I'll never know. Because he could never get the words out.

The whole semester was a series of me bringing up the fact he was becoming distant, and him sitting in silence. I even asked if he thought we should have an open relationship, or even take a break. I thought these suggestions would shock him into saying something, but he just stared back at me blankly. Every single time. Not a fucking word.

He didn't want to break my heart, but he *was*—in a slower, more insidious way.

My friends had been trying to tell me that semester maybe he was gaslighting me, maybe he wasn't all I cracked him up to be; maybe he was being emotionally abusive. And my personal favorite: maybe he was the Roy to my Jim from *The Office*. But I was quick to remind them they had never been in such a long-term relationship and they didn't know what they were talking about.

I wish I could have been stronger. I wish I could have seen what was happening. But I was holding on with white knuckles to the rose-colored Candy Land universe we used to walk through together. I was holding onto a white picket fence future.

Later that night, as I lay squished up in a ball on Jonah's couch, I texted Yes Man.

"Do you still love me?" I pressed send. That was probably the most vulnerable text I have ever sent.

"I think so . . . But it's getting hard to remember why."

I flew back home to St. Louis the next day. It was cold, dark, and raining. On my uber ride back to campus, I asked the driver to drop me off on the Loop instead. The Loop is a street near WashU with a bunch of cool restaurants, stores, and piercing shops. The driver dropped me off at Enigma Piercings and Tattoos.

I went in and got my cartilage pierced. It bled so much when he jabbed the needle into me. Blood ran down my ear and onto my neck. It hurt so fucking badly. But my face didn't budge. I was numb and I wanted to change who I was. I wanted to be someone Yes Man would pay attention to. I wanted to be edgy. I wanted to be chill. I wanted to be the type of girlfriend who was okay with my boyfriend fucking around with his frat and lying to me about it.

But I wasn't any of those things and I knew it.

Black Mold

May 15, 2019

Age 20, summer after sophomore year of college

Sixteen days and I'm off to NYC for the summer. Three more days and Yes Man is off to Israel for Birthright. He's not even Jewish; he just wants to go party in Tel Aviv? Like, what?

He lied to me yesterday. Again. We were supposed to hang out because we only have a few days before we are apart for the summer. He didn't answer his phone all day. We were supposed to hang out, but he was MIA. I found out, by checking his friends' snapchat stories, that he was tripping. Again.

I was very angry and sad. I went over to his house today and was just silent. He tried hugging me when I got there, and I couldn't bring myself to hug him back. We lay on his bed and stared at each other silently. It was weird. I don't know. I was really confused and sad.

"Do you resent me?" I asked.

"I don't know. Why else would I have lied to you? I keep lying to you," he said. His face looked like a sad puppy. He knew he was screwing up and he looked guilty. I felt bad for him.

"I feel like," I stared at the ground. "That by staying with you . . . I'm not respecting myself. Like, . . . now I'm one of those girls who lets her boyfriend lie to her and stays with him anyway. That's not me." The words burned as they left my mouth. Truth hurts.

"I know," he breathed out.

We're both sick of these talks. I'm sick of writing about it. Honestly, I wish I had something meaningful to say. I mean, I'm literally moving to New York City in two weeks but I can't even be excited because I'm so anxious about my boyfriend. How did I get here? Remember when I said I would never have a boyfriend in high school? Fuck me.

"You put a lot of pressure on me," he said. "To see our future together. My mind doesn't work like that. You have all these visions about what you want your life to look like, and I'm in that vision. But I can't think like that. I have no idea what's going to happen."

We both just stared at the ceiling. My body got that tingly black out feeling where panic starts to push reality away. I need to stop having these talks with him. I need to quit making this relationship contingent on if we get married or not. It's fucked up how much I think about it. It's just comforting, because the thought of loving someone this much only to have my heart be brutally ripped out of my chest is terrifying, to say the least. It's fucked up. I need to just let him go. I need to go and do my own thing. But being together is still the best feeling in the world.

"I'm scared," I said. "I don't want to break up."

"Me neither."

We fell asleep. When we woke up, we went back to pretending that everything was normal.

I never heard back from *Late Night*, but I did get a job in NBC's Cable Entertainment department working for the Syfy network! It felt like a miracle! I still watch my Snapchat memories from the day I got the phone call when they offered me the job. I ran around my dorm room dancing to "P.I.M.P." by 50 Cent and giggling ferociously. Those seventy-six emails to WashU alumni had paid off. I was so proud of myself and excited for a summer in The Big City. I forgot to even tell Yes Man until days later. We had been mutually avoiding each other because any time we would hang out, we had long, terrible talks where we would both inadvertently admit how stuck we felt in our high school romance we were clearly outgrowing.

Finding an apartment in New York so last minute was an absolute nightmare. I found out about my job on May 7 and had to be in New York on May 31. Entertainment is so careless like that. I wound up finding a tiny studio apartment with my friend Sophia. She also had a job in Manhattan for the summer, and she was dating Dance Man. I had set them up.

It was so expensive. My parents almost had a heart attack when I told them how much rent was going to be, but my dad was adamant I go anyway. I split the rent with my parents, and it was every bit of every penny I made the whole summer. Technically, I was only paying a fourth because I was also splitting rent with Sophia, and it still drained my bank account. Sophia and I shared a queen-sized bed in a tiny room that was smaller than my bedroom in Imperial . . . for the entire summer.

When I arrived at our apartment by myself with two big suitcases, the landlord called Sophia and told her it had flooded, and we had to stay somewhere else until it was fixed. *God, I love this city*, I thought, a little more ironically this time. The landlord let us stay in another empty room for two nights.

That first weekend, Sophia and I went to the Governor's Ball music festival. She is very short, just like me, but we pushed and shoved our way to the very front for the Florence and the Machine concert. We were right in the front, slammed up against the gate they put up to contain everyone.

That concert felt like the first moment I had finally stepped into the manifestation I had conjured up in my head, sitting in my backyard in Imperial. I was at a concert. In New York City. With a job at NBC, where I would get to push past the tourists with their selfie sticks and walk into 30 Rock every day and scan my badge into the endless elevator banks. I had made it, and it was—is— only the beginning.

When Florence sang "Dog Days Are Over", I threw my head back and screamed the words, tears falling out of my eyes and my heart swelling up with excitement but also pain. I wanted to run fast and let it all go like she was singing. She looked so free on stage, spinning in circles with her crazy red hair flying around her. Part of me felt free like I was finally getting out. But part of me felt so, so stuck. She sang about leaving things behind. I knew I needed to. But I just—

Didn't know how.

I woke up early for my first day of work because I thought I heard water running. I rubbed my eyes open and sat up slowly and looked down at the floor and screamed.

"*Sophia!*" I shrieked. "*Ah! Fuck!*" Our bathroom had flooded overnight. Again. And it wasn't just water. Our bed was *surrounded* by a moat of shit. Literal shit. It was steadily flowing out from under the bathroom door, and it wasn't stopping! Sophia jolted out of bed, naked. She slept naked every night. This was news to me on our first night. The number of times I rolled over in the middle of the night to a nipple in my face is a testament to my love and dedication to the Small Girl, Big City dream.

"*Oh my god!*" Sophia and I sprang up onto our feet and were jumping on our bed, holding onto each other, staring down at our entire apartment floor, flooded with *inches* of smelly, brown water that kept bubbling out from under the bathroom door.

"Do we just leave?" I shouted.

"Yes! We have to!" Sophia yelled back. Luckily, our closet was smashed up next to the bed so we both leaned in and frantically yanked clothes off of hangers. I'll never forget pulling our pants on as we jumped on top of that queen bed before our first days of work in "The Big City," surrounded by a flood of our own shit.

We leaped off of the bed, snagged our shoes from the floor, and ran out of the door. My hair was the greasiest it has ever been and I forgot to grab underwear. My shoes were only a little damp with shit water. Sophia and I stared at each other in the hallway, out of breath, and walked to the elevator.

"Like ... I guess we just go to work? Call the landlord?" I wondered out loud, glancing at my greasy reflection in the elevator mirror, realizing my clothes didn't match. She nodded and we went to work.

The shit water moat taught me you can prepare for something so much and take all the right precautions and perform all the right rituals to prepare yourself for a big day, and in the end, shit is out of your control. Literally. My own shit was out of control.

But everything always seems to work out anyway. I had a great first day at NBC and learned I can totally pull off a slicked back bun that appears sleek and high fashion but is actually just greasy. I have since utilized this look several times.

We went to work and someone came to fix our apartment. It all appeared fine and dandy, but a few weeks later, I woke up in the middle of the night with a fever and shakes and started throwing up. We later found out there was black mold growing in our floorboards and I had gotten sick from it. After that, our landlord's company moved us to another apartment. I came home from work that night around ten o'clock, and Sophia and I packed everything up and dragged it to another building around midnight.

This new building on first Avenue and thirty-fourth Street was astonishingly swanky. It was luxury. We walked into the lobby with vaulted ceilings and marble walls with big chandeliers and waterfalls and gasped, mouths gaping open. Our landlord's company wasn't charging us extra because we had made a big fit about the fact I had been puking and missing work from the black mold. Even though we still had to share a bed, the new swanky building was totally worth it.

I had more friends in New York City that summer than I did back home in St. Louis. A lot of people from K.A.R.L.—current members and alumni—were living in the city. Not to mention, a lot of WashU kids are from the city originally, so they were there too. On Sundays, my K.A.R.L. friends and I would meet at Upright Citizens Brigade and watch ASSSSCAT, which is a famous weekly improv show Amy Poehler's improv troupe started. It was the best part of my week. Since I lived right on the East River, I'd ride the ferry back and forth from Brooklyn just for fun on the weekends. It was like a cheap boat ride! (But I stopped when I realized it was just me and the same four homeless dudes drinking out of brown paper bags who did this every weekend.)

In my new fancy apartment I was paying very little for, I pretended to be a successful, Forbes 30 Under 30 Millennial. I found myself inviting all my friends from K.A.R.L., NBC, and WashU over to have pizza and wine on the sexy rooftop every weekend. I absolutely loved having a place to host a big group of people. I adored introducing school friends to work friends and watching people get along. After growing up so far away from friends, having my own apartment in a central location was a dream come true.

On the other hand, NBC was . . . boring. The idea of it was exciting—don't get me wrong. I got butterflies every time I walked through those revolving doors or marched up the stairs from the Rockefeller Center subway stop. But the job itself was boring, and surprisingly very corporate.

"So when do we get to go on set?" My fellow intern Josh asked on our first day. Our manager laughed.

"Oh!" She chuckled. "No, there's no sets here. We don't make the shows. We hire production companies to do that." She said it like it was obvious, but to three wide-eyed interns hoping to get their feet wet and see the nitty gritty behind-the-scenes of TV shows, it was a bit devastating. You could see all of our shoulders slump and we turned to each other with concerned looks. *So what would we be doing all summer?*

Turns out we would be sitting at a desk organizing computer files and doing prop runs over the city to find incredibly niche items like beige bodysuits with arms and legs, creepy baby dolls, limited edition action figures from the 1950s, and glow in the dark cake icing. We would clean out costume closets and deliver mail to the Bravo and Oxygen floors. One day, I picked up Andy Cohen's mail—a fellow St. Louisan! I was so excited to deliver it to his office! But he wasn't there that day.

Truth be told, most days I sat at my desk clicking and dragging files, and counting down the hours until six o'clock. I was ready to work and get my hands dirty, but there just wasn't much for us to do.

Syfy had cancelled their top three biggest shows the week the interns arrived. Even our managers were working for the USA Network instead of Syfy. Another bummer: Syfy didn't have room for the interns on their floor, so myself and the other two Syfy interns sat on the legal affairs floor. We had to whisper because the one time we actually started chatting, the lawyer behind us made a phone call to our manager and we had a *talking to* about how we had to stay quiet.

But even the Syfy floor was nearly silent. Everyone sat in cubicles with headphones, hunched over their keyboards. If people were chatting at each other's desks, it was in hushed tones. Even the heads of the department had tiny, closet offices with no windows. The other interns and myself were surprised by this.

We were all creative people, hungry to express ourselves and collaborate with others. In my head, everyone had been whisking around in pretty colors, making jokes with their colleagues, running back and forth with movie posters and alien costumes, shouting across the floor there was an emergency meeting about a commercial airing that night, and walking in and out of big, glass corner offices that overlooked the city.

But it might as well have been an accounting firm for all anyone knew. It was quiet and stale. The ceilings were low, the cubicles were crammed, and the walls and floors were gray. I don't think "quiet and stale" was the case for NBC interns in other departments though. Our manager apologized for not having more work for us to do that summer. They couldn't have anticipated the cancelling of three shows.

So this left me with lots of time to sit at my unanticipated corporate desk job and be anxious about Yes Man, who had not texted me once since I had gotten to New York. Here I was living a dream come true, and I wasn't sharing any of it with my boyfriend of almost four years.

I remember walking home from work one day in the rain with an umbrella. A guy walking in front of me stopped in front of a street vendor and bought a bouquet of flowers. I started tearing up. *What?* I was surprised by my reaction. *Why was I so sad? Why did a man getting someone flowers feel so heartbreaking?* It felt like a rock was dropped on my chest. I kept walking home. My throat was tight and threatening to erupt into a sob. *Because Yes Man wouldn't do that for me,* I realized. The truth was so heavy and dark, just like the dark clouds hanging over the city that day.

That whole summer was a strange dichotomy between finally feeling free, living my dreams, being proud of myself, hanging out with awesome people, going to cool restaurants and comedy shows, working at my dream company, having pizza on my sexy rooftop, . . . and feeling like an absolute wreck on the inside.

My heart was slowly breaking and I was doing everything in my power to pretend it wasn't. I was also walking to work every day in a sea of attractive men in navy blue suits and ties and long, shiny brown shoes. I remember wanting to flirt with them and go on dates with them, and sometimes I would stand next to them on the subway and hope they would just look at me, I guess. They never did. They all had AirPods in and were checking the NASDAQ on their phones.

Being in New York City made me realize I was really silly for wanting to marry my high school sweetheart.

There was a massive, exciting, vibrant, and wild world out here! *Was I really going to lock things down with the first boy I had ever dated?* Where was the fun in *that*? Suddenly, a surprising lure to the single life approached my precious little imagined bubble of married at twenty-three and kids at twenty-six. Suddenly, I was confused.

I started going to SoulCycle. I know, go ahead and roll your eyes. (For those who don't know, SoulCycle is a spin class with a cult-like motivational speaking twist.) I only went three or four times, but honestly, there *was* something kind of spiritual about it. I would sit at a desk for eight hours, repeatedly checking my phone to see if Yes Man had answered a Snapchat—which he rarely did—and get up and go to the bathroom and wipe my armpits with toilet paper because they were sweaty with anxiety. Then, I would leave work and take the subway somewhere I could shake the day off. I walked into the black room with endless stationary bikes and pedaled my goddamn heart out.

The instructors would shout aggressively empowering things like, "You're stronger than you know!" and "Throw negativity out of your life!" and *"Fuck yes, we are free!"* And I would squint my eyes through the sweat, bow my head down, and pedal all of my anxious energy out; giving it all I had and hoping I *was* stronger than I knew.

One night, Sophia and I got into a passive aggressive argument about who was paying more for groceries. (She definitely was, and I feel shitty about it now. I was being a careless roommate at SoulCycle and ASSSSCAT, running from my problems.) She let it slip somewhere in the conversation she knew why Yes Man wasn't answering me.

Yes Man, while he was partying in Tel Aviv pretending to be Jewish, admitted to Sophia and I's mutual friend, Rachel, he wanted to break up with me, but he didn't know how. Rachel told Sophia and she had known about it the entire summer. It was July at this point. Sophia burst into a full-blown panic attack when she told me. I, on the other hand, stood eerily still and took a very slow sip of water as I watched her hyperventilate and cry on the floor.

"I'm *so* sorry!" she wailed. I was frozen. It was weird. *Why the hell was* she *freaking out?*

"No." I took a sip of water. I was standing in the bathroom doorway. "It's okay." I turned around and went to bed, numb and unsurprised.

The next day at work, I was suspiciously happy. I think they call it manic. Yep. *That.* I was smiling ear to ear and talking really loudly at lunch and laughing breathy, forced laughs. I went to SoulCycle after work. It was a typical, intense sweat session. But then, the last song came on and it was Florence and the Machine's "Dog Days Are Over" remixed with Drake's "Over."

The faint ukulele melody began to play and my heart skipped a beat. It was like the Universe, or God, or whoever, was taking me by the shoulders, shaking me, saying, "*Kelly! It's time to* let go! *It's* over!"

I took a deep breath and bowed my head. I started pedaling. I cranked the resistance up really high. I wanted to feel it burn. I started going faster. The chorus arrived, and I was off. I was sprinting. I pounded my legs into those pedals, spinning my feet as fast as they would go, and breathing hard, exhausted breaths.

I closed my eyes and went faster, sweat running down my face, stinging as it reached my eyes. The emotional weight was getting heavier as my legs got tired. My chest swelled up, and in between breaths, I started to cry, tears mixing in with the sweat on my face and dripping off my chin onto the bike.

Release. Yep. *That's* what it was.

I got off the bike and let out a massive breath. The air felt tingly and oddly present. I took a cold shower in the locker room. I rode the M17 bus back home. Later that night, after Sophia had went to bed, I walked out onto our couch in the next room over. *This had to happen now.* I FaceTimed Yes Man on my laptop.

"What's up?" he answered, not smiling.

"Hi...." My voice was shaky. *Was I really going to do it?* "How are you?" I asked, attempting to make small talk.

"Fine," he mumbled, not looking into the camera. I took a deep breath. I couldn't beat around this bush any longer.

"So," I breathed out shakily, "Do you think we should break up?" My words hung, suspended in midair. I held my breath. He looked back into the camera, but he didn't look surprised at all.

"Yeah, ..." he sighed, defeated.

And just like that, on a couch in Manhattan, the nearly four-year relationship I had naively invested my entire future into broke. Shattered like glass on the floor. Disappeared like a ghost. Evaporated into thin air like smoke in a wildfire.

The silence that came after ran through my chest like a train. I was winded. Though I wasn't surprised, the reality of it punched me in the gut.

"Okay," I said, finally catching my breath. "So . . . That's it then?"

"Yeah. . . . I guess. . . ." He looked away from the camera, biting his barely-quivering lip.

"Can't we just wait until next semester when I go abroad? I don't wanna deal with this at school," I pleaded. I see now how ridiculous this was. I cared less about losing him and more about what my life would look like at school. My friends were his frat friends, and he had custody over them. I was out.

"No, Kelly," he whispered. "You know we have to do this now. . . . And you'll be okay."

I looked across my apartment, my eyes suddenly crystal clear, and watched my carefully crafted vision of the future dissipate into nothingness. We were silent for a while.

But we looked back at each other on FaceTime and started laughing a little bit. *Lovers smile when they break up*, a professor once said to me.

Maybe we laughed in awe, maybe out of relief? It felt like a veil had been lifted and we were finally able to speak to each other again. We talked about how we had been feeling and how we both knew this was the right decision for months but weren't strong enough to do it, to pull the trigger. It was both of our first love, our first long relationship, our first breakup. We knew for a while we had to do it, and it was straining both of us. But now we were on the same page again, and we both agreed we needed to move on.

We talked for a while. I went to the bathroom in the middle of our conversation, and when I sat down to pee, I smiled a big smile, still wiping tears off my face. *Wow.* A whole world of possibilities appeared in my mind. A thousand doors opened; it's almost like I felt it! The unknown had never felt so calm and inviting. Who would have guessed? For someone who had been planning every minute of her life out, to not have any clue what was going to happen for once was so fucking exhilarating.

I was incredibly heartbroken, and I knew what was to follow this would be an absolute train wreck, but I was so excited.

The Saddest Part

———

July 28, 2019

Age 20, summer in New York City

The part that makes my stomach flip the most and takes my breath away is the fact that I let myself be treated like shit for so long. I let myself get hurt over and over again. I'm not mad and I don't blame myself—I hold a lot of compassion for myself.

Ironically, while everything was falling apart, I had the audacity to give other people advice on their relationships. Meanwhile, I was telling myself so many lies about what was actually going on in mine. Way, way back, buried somewhere deep within my subconscious, I knew things were unhealthy and bad, but I convinced myself that it was all okay. I told myself that our issues were solvable. And hey, maybe they were. But problems in a relationship can only be fixed by both people, and I was the only one holding a hammer. He was playing beer pong.

The saddest part is that when I entered this relationship, I knew exactly who I was, which is probably why it started out so great. And I would go around saying wise shit like, "Don't enter a relationship until you understand who you are, what you're worth, and you know how to ask for what you deserve." Like thank you, sixteen-year-old Oprah. But college shakes things up.

People say, "college changes people". I agree to an extent. I think college changes dynamics between people. People are put into situations they were never in before and they make decisions they've never made before, and that changes things.

During all of these shifting dynamics, I lost who I was. The person I loved more than anything in the world was actively and persistently pushing me away. To me, that could only mean that something in me had changed, or that I had suddenly become unattractive to him, and that it was up to me to get on his level and be worthy of the love I used to receive from him.

I stopped getting replies to texts. My calls went unanswered. I would spend my Friday nights on Rachel's couch waiting for him to reply to one of my hundred texts about what his plans were for the night. At midnight, Rachel would leave to go see her boyfriend. I would go up to my room, get high, and go to bed.

I would wake up on Saturday mornings to find snap stories of Yes Man drunk off his ass at a bar. I would wake up on Saturday mornings with no texts back, usually because his phone had "died", which I always forgave him for the second he finally replied.

One night, he got so plastered that he threw up in the Uber (during which time I so graciously held the barf bag open), rolled out into the street unconscious, got EST called on him, and then got up and ran all the way back to his frat and climbed into bed. Some guys in his frat, a lot of guys actually, were trying to take care of him. I stood there and sobbed, embarrassed that I was dating such an immature, gross frat guy who even other frat guys thought was sloppy. And he was the fucking president of this frat. How embarrassing. The next day, I told all my friends the story like it was the funniest thing ever. They saw right through me.

At his fraternity formal, he won the superlative, "most likely to wake up naked in the chapter room and be found by maintenance". I was so embarrassed, but I laughed and hugged him anyway. In that moment, I realized I was dating a very different person than I thought I was. No one wants to date that guy.

That spring semester, he maybe slept over five to seven times. Most times he came over, it would be the middle of the night. He would be drunk and would pass out all sweaty, would take up the whole bed, and I would stay awake with my eyes wide open wondering who I needed to become for him to stop treating me with such disinterest and disrespect.

When he lied to me for the third time, I knew that the logical thing to do was dump his ass. He knew it too. I saw him realize what a piece of shit he was. I felt it in my heart; the damage was done. It was over in that moment. I wanted to end it right there so badly, but in the moment, when I sat on his bed and stared at him helplessly with tears flowing down my face while he stared back blankly, the fear of what my life would be like without him washed over me. I lurched forward, clung to him and cried, "I can't live without you!"

Turns out, I'm living more than I ever have without him.

The saddest part is that I abandoned all that I stood for. I compromised my integrity. I made decisions I wasn't ready to make because I thought I had to for him. I surrendered to being with someone who continually lied to me, who did not prioritize me, who questioned my beliefs, who blew off mental health as a hoax for the weak, and who did not communicate with me in any regard.

I lied and told myself that these problems were temporary. Even more sickening, I slowly began to accept that my life's partner just wouldn't be my perfect match. I started gearing up, subconsciously, for a life of coming home to a dirty kitchen and a husband watching TV and ignoring me. And for what? Security? That's my guess. Well, that, and love. Haha! How short did I think life was?

When you love someone, you give up the right to see things clearly. Don't worry, it's not immediate. But when it's been nearly four years, you don't know the difference between making decisions for yourself and making decisions for your relationship.

At least, that was my problem. It definitely wasn't his problem because in the end, he was never making any decisions about our relationship. He let me hammer nail after nail after nail and never offered to help. He never even offered to look around and see the progress I thought I was making, no matter how many times I cried and dragged him by his ankles to come help me fix the mess he so recklessly and carelessly made. That's probably what pushed him away too. I was trying too hard.

The minute we broke up, my rose-colored glasses fell off and shattered on the floor. The weights wrapped around my ankles rolled away into the corner. My tightly-wound, carefully-curated vision of my future dissolved before my eyes. Then I went to bed.

The next morning, I walked around my apartment in the fresh morning sun, and I stretched my arms out above my head and let out a highly-anticipated, long-awaited, well-deserved sigh of relief. The fight was over.

It was the first time I woke up at peace, and not in anxiety's nauseating death grip, in months. That's when I cried the most.

I had wept when I realized that the breakup didn't hurt, but it was the thought of the past year that truly brought me to my knees.

I sobbed—not at the thought of losing him, but realizing that I had wronged myself as much as he had wronged me.

I was reunited with myself that morning. It felt like I was getting the biggest hug in the world from myself. I've never felt a wave of compassion as strong as that. And that's the saddest part.

For the previous eight months, I had been struggling with an onslaught of anxiety that I had never experienced before. I went to therapy once, and I talked about stupid shit like high school and my family, but that wasn't the issue. I remember sitting in the session and feeling a rising panic when she asked about my boyfriend. I remember shoving it down and smiling and saying, "no, he's great. He's not the problem."

There were nights I didn't sleep at all. Literally. Like I know people say they didn't sleep all night, but there was one night when I actually did not. I lay in bed and my heart was pounding—no, vibrating—out of my chest. I could hardly breathe. I was having a panic attack, but it was the middle of the night and I didn't want to wake up my suitemates. I didn't want help.

I was having a panic attack because he didn't text me back, and I knew he didn't love me the way he used to, and I knew that I wasn't going to admit that, and I knew that I wasn't going to break up with him because I was scared to give up the vision of my safe, secure future with him. I have panic attacks when I feel stuck.

There were many nights, and mornings, along this same tone. Sometimes he would even be sleeping over and I would get up and cry silently on the floor. In the mornings, he would leave and I wouldn't know the next time I'd see him, despite asking him when he was free. "I don't know," he'd say.

I told him so many times: "I'm just really anxious this semester. It's like the weather or something; I think I have something seasonal." My classes were hard, but I dropped one within the first couple weeks, so that stopped being the problem. Summer came, and I was still anxious and insecure about myself, and I thought it was just me going through some self-discovery issues. Because he was out doing whip-its, poppers, molly, and acid, I thought I should be piercing my nose, getting tattoos, snorting Adderall, and buying my own weed for the first time.

On one of our few days together before I left for New York, I cried to him in the car and said, "If I was in Pi Phi and did a ton of drugs, then you would love me more!"

How fucked up. I really believed that shit.

I spent three fourths of my summer in New York reflecting on myself, and trying to get rid of my anxiety—not for me, but for him—so that when I came home, he would see a new, carefree Kelly that he felt comfortable doing drugs in front of.

I read some self-help books about acceptance and a bunch of other bullshit. I tried to work out more so I could look hotter for him when I got back. I thought about getting a tattoo to show him that I could change too, like he was.

That morning when I walked into the living room and the sun washed over me, it was all gone. I breathed out and realized that I didn't want to dye my hair black, I never liked doing coke or Adderall, I didn't want to trip acid, and I actually didn't like the guys in his frat that much. They're all a bunch of lost souls, gassing each other up and getting more lost in the ephemeral veil of drugs and cool tapestries.

I realized that I was not the cause of my anxiety: he was. I realized that I love exactly who I am, and I don't need to change a goddamn thing for anyone.

I walked into the bathroom and washed my face. I looked in the mirror while I wiped my face with a towel. I realized in that moment that it had been a long, long, long time since I had made a decision for myself.

Ashes to Ashes

———

"Well, don't sit in bed and cry," my mom said over the phone the next morning as I looked at my puffy eyes in my Snapchat camera. "You have to get up. Go into the city and do stuff. I don't care what, but you can't sit in bed and cry all day."

I listened to her, and thank God I did. Maybe it was my mom's tough love, or maybe it was the years of cheerleading that told me when you get dropped on your ass, you get back up and put on a hell of a show with sequins and red lipstick. So that's what I did. I had three weeks left in New York City to be Single Kelly. I could figure out the deep shit later.

I downloaded Hinge and off I went! I chased those sexy, city-slicker, Navy-Blue Suit Men. I went on date after date after date. I was wined and dined with the financial analysts, the real estate brokers, the law students—you name it. I was putting on lipstick in the bathroom at NBC and rushing downstairs to the 30 Rock subway in tight jeans and heels to meet men for happy hours on fancy rooftops. I was manically fearless with no time to waste.

"Don't you think you're moving on pretty quickly?" Sophia nervously asked me one night.

"Nope."

In an ironic way, after having grown up watching movies about people falling in love in New York City, it only felt right to have my heart broken there. Though it was incredibly painful, it also felt romantic and exhilarating to step into the world as Single Kelly on the streets of Manhattan.

It was only a few days after the breakup when I got a tattoo. I felt reckless and free. When Koky jabbed the needle into my arm, I felt powerful and in control. I wanted to make a massive decision for *me*. The tattoo is very small and it says, "yes, and"; a cliché improv tattoo. I drunkenly texted my parents a long paragraph that went something along the lines of *"this is not a phase!"* It very well may be a phase, but so be it.

I was riding such a high those last three weeks in the city. I was finally enjoying it the way I should have been all summer. I saw a lot of WashU friends, K.A.R.L. friends, and met a lot of handsome guys who paid for a lot of nice dinners. Sage took me on a weekend road trip to Newport, Rhode Island. I felt amazing, and I was so excited to go on this new journey of "finding myself" and then—

Bam. The plane landed back in St. Louis. Reality started to sink in; hard.

I was anxious to start the fall semester of my junior year. I had only a few friends who weren't in Yes Man's fraternity. Even the girls I had formed friendships with were just other girlfriends of those guys. I had lots of surface level friends sprinkled around, but no one who I trusted enough to lend me a shoulder to cry on. I wasn't used to relying on anyone besides Yes Man for those moments: a big mistake.

On the first day of school, I was carrying up a box to my apartment on campus and I ran into my friend Andy.

"Kelly! You're living in this building too! Guess I'll be seeing a lot of Yes Man around!" *Goddamnit*, I thought. *How many more times was this going to happen?*

"Uhm," I stuttered, the box in my arms got heavier as I stood on the steps. "We broke up." *Bam.* Reality slapped me in the face. I never thought I'd utter those words on WashU's campus, but there I was, standing corrected.

"Oh! *Real nice, Andy!* Jeez!" Andy's friend yelled from inside. Andy gave me an awkward smile and walked away.

I got settled into my room and was feeling optimistic. I was excited to finally flirt with boys at bars and dance at other fraternities. I couldn't wait to finally go out with the girls and take tequila shots and dance together all night.

But these fantasies came to a screeching halt when a girl bumped into me at a bar, gave me a big smile, and grabbed Yes Man by his shirt and started making out with him.

The room started spinning. I started seeing black spots here and there. My ears started ringing and the music faded out. I was in the middle of flirting with a guy at the bar and had completely forgotten he was standing next to me. It felt like a bad dream, and my mind was struggling to wrap itself around the reality of this nightmare.

"—Maybe next weekend?" The guy's voice faded back in.

"Oh! Uh. . . . Sorry, what was that?" I blinked a few times, smiled, and took a sip of my drink. My head was pounding. I felt lightheaded. I wanted to go home immediately. I was devastated.

It never occurred to me something this horrendous was possible now. It wasn't just a new world with Single Kelly. Single Yes Man was in this world too, and we were in *very* close quarters. WashU is not very big. I thought if anyone was going to move on quickly, it would be me. I didn't even fathom the possibility he could have gotten a new girlfriend—or whatever their deal was—in the first month of school. I felt pathetic and worthless, like my role in our four-year relationship was effortlessly replaceable.

I continued to see these two together most times I went out and during the day on campus. It made me sick to my stomach. It felt disrespectful in a way. I know it's not a *fair* feeling to feel. He wasn't mine anymore, but that's how it felt. It was also embarrassing. After months of wondering who I needed to become for Yes Man to show interest, the answer bumped into me at the bar. She fit perfectly into Yes Man's new life. She was what I feared he wanted me to morph into, and it sucked to be right.

My visions of taking tequila shots and dancing with "the girls" to Lizzo songs also came to a screeching halt when I realized my two roommates were dating guys in Yes Man's fraternity (that I had set them up with) and they spent their weekends with their boyfriends. All of the female friend groups I knew about through my sorority or elsewhere were already formed. By junior year, it seemed like everyone had a solid circle of friends and wasn't looking to add any members. I tried going out with a couple different groups, but I didn't have friendships that came anywhere close to filling the new void within me.

I felt completely stranded. I had no idea who I was, and it was terrifying. I didn't know who I wanted to even associate with. My roommates, who I thought were my closest friends, had no idea what I was going through and neither did I.

My roommates got sick and tired of my manic mood swings and quickly shut me out. I don't blame them, but it would have been nice to have people around me who knew what it was like to go through a gut-wrenching heartbreak. I didn't know what to expect of myself. I didn't know how I was going to react. Turns out, it wasn't pretty.

By mid-November, I was spiraling hard, but smiling through the pain—in denial of how broken and clueless I was.

November 18, 2019

Age 20, junior year of college

I feel so bitter and angry and tense. I think I am doing well, but I think I put on a really tough face because I want everyone to see how well I'm doing and I want people to think I'm strong. "External validation." "Obsession with the appearance of success." This is what my enneagram says. How gross is that.

I've been taking personality tests all week when I get bored. Why? Probably because I'm feeling lost and I don't know who I am and I'm searching to reconnect with a deeper meaning of what it means to be me.

All I know is that I know who I am, but I also don't have a clue who I am! Am I edgy because I have a tattoo? Do I work hard because I have such a deep inner shame that I need to prove myself to others and receive external validation to feel worthy? What are my values? Do I believe in God? Am I one of those girls that smokes weed? Or someone that doesn't? Do I like casual hook ups or do I want to wait until I fall in love again?! Am I straight or did I actually want to make out with that girl at the bar? Do I believe in self-discipline and working hard? Or do I believe in relaxing and enjoying life and trusting that things will work out? Am I liberal? Am I conservative? I don't know! FUCK.

Okay, now I just have to laugh. I think this is just what growing up means.

I felt like I was in a tornado. School, friends, roommates, parties, boys, fear; I was a train-wreck.

My mom drove to WashU after work one day and picked me up to take me home. I walked into my house and collapsed onto my living room floor and started sobbing. My parents looked at me lovingly, but clearly concerned.

"What's wrong, sweetie?" my dad said softly. *Agh. Fuck. Everything.* How do you explain to your parents there's nothing they can do? You're just *sad*. Your insides hurt. Your head is all over the place. You wake up every day and wonder, *when will I be okay again?* And people say, "it just takes time," and you wonder, *well, how much?*

One night, when I saw Yes Man and New Girlfriend out at a bar, I really started spinning. I grabbed my friend's arm and just blurted out, "I'm not okay." Her eyes bore into mine and she nodded. We tried dancing and I remember my body moving up and down but I didn't feel anything. I was silent in the Uber ride home, my eyes glued open, holding my breath. I was so focused on not losing it. I just had to wait a few more minutes until I could get to my room and then—

"*Ah!*" I screamed into my pillows, punched my mattress, clawed my sheets, and sobbed with white knuckles while I hyperventilated into my bedspread. I ripped all of the sheets off my bed and fell onto my floor. I cried heavily for hours—probably three. I was in so much pain. My chest hurt and my blood was boiling and there was nothing I could do to soothe it. It was agony; there's no other way to describe it. It sounds dramatic, and it was. I was hurting. Badly.

Sometimes you just fucking lose it.

I couldn't sleep one night because my chest hurt so badly and I was having trouble breathing. *No, I'm fine*, I kept thinking to myself. I got up and ate dry Cheerios in the living room and watched *The Office* from four to six in the morning. I never do stuff like this. I felt like I was going to die if I went back to bed. I waited until I felt safe enough to close my eyes, and I woke up at seven-thirty to go down to the studio for another eighteen-hour day.

I was running the gauntlet, man. WashU is hard enough as it is. The workload itself will send any sane person into an out-of-body experience. Adding anything on top of that will nearly kill you.

Every day, I walked up a massive staircase from my apartment up to campus. Every day was its own battle. Every day I wondered, *how much longer?* Every night, I curled into a ball in my bed and hugged myself tightly. "You're okay," I whispered over and over again until I fell asleep.

This all sounds so depressing and psychotic and sad and terrible and to be honest with you, I hate writing about it. It's embarrassing. *All this? Really? I was twenty years old and broke up with my boyfriend—it's not that big of a deal!* It was though.

It wasn't just a breakup. I lost the version of a life I thought I was going to live. I lost the control I thought I had over my future. I lost what I thought my identity was. I broke up with a version of myself.

I'm obviously pulling out the most poignant moments for the sake of writing but also because this is the shit nobody sees that happens behind closed doors. Humans do weird shit. This is the shit people do when they are hurting. This is the shit you only know about if your heart has been ripped out of your chest. This is the shit you don't tell people about because you don't want them to worry about you. This is the day-to-day shit that happens when you're *going through something.* This is the shit you think about when people ask, "how are you?" and you reply, "good!" with a fake, breathy smile.

Halfway through the semester, my roommates, Sophia and Rachel, sat me down for what can only be defined as an intervention. But it wasn't one that started with, "we love you and we're worried about you." No. It was a laundry list of my character flaws.

"We think you might be a narcissist." Wow. The words still burn, and I still talk about them in my student-discount therapy sessions. "When you talk about boys and how hot you think you are, it makes us feel insecure, and we need emotional space from you." This list went on for three more hours.

I sat on a kitchen chair and just stared at them. My heart was pounding. *Was this really happening?* I was spinning in the winds of my own tornado. I had no idea I was affecting others. I was so caught up with the deafening static noise in my own head I wasn't thinking for a second about anyone else.

"I'm sorry. I guess I'm just a bad person . . ." I guessed out loud. I didn't know how to fix what they were saying. I had no idea what I was doing wrong. I felt my mind turn inside out as I started to contemplate maybe I was the villain all along. I was so weak and lost I didn't have it in me to stand up for myself. I didn't trust I was good. They said I was bad, and I didn't know what the fuck I was. So I believed them.

That conversation lit something up within me. I was so confused. *Was that really how I was behaving? Was I really hurting people in the wake of my mess? Was I really just inherently bad?* I started to journal.

October 22, 2019

Age 20, junior year of college

I am going to change. I am going to be better. I am going to stop focusing so much on boys. I am going to try and not talk bad about people. I am going to think more about what I say before I say it. I'm going to do my best to be honest about what I'm feeling instead of pretending to be strong. I can be strong and sad at the same time.

I've been sprinting away. I'm afraid of being sad. I feel like a loose cannon.

I have a lot to learn about what it means to be honest with others, but also myself. I have a lot of work to do to rebuild a foundation of self-esteem. I have a lot of work to do on trusting myself and my friends. I think that being honest and open to big changes will lead to authentic growth.

On my last night in that apartment, I found out my roommates had gotten hold of my diary, which was unfortunately on my Google Drive, and read it.

Note: Do *not* put your diary online and expect nothing bad to happen.

My friend Sutton came to me about it, laughing. "You'll never believe what I heard! It's so ridiculous! Someone was telling people in Kyle's frat that your roommates read your diary! Ha! People love to just make stuff up!"

As soon as she said it, I knew it was true. I had a gut-twisting feeling the way my roommates had been tip-toeing around me the last week was not a coincidence.

Rachel came home that night and sat next to me on the couch. My heart was racing. I had to just *ask*.

"I have to ask you something, and it's really crazy," I said nervously, and boy, did she look scared.

"Okay," she said. I couldn't believe what I was about to ask.

"Did you read my diary?" I could hear my heart pounding.

"Yes," she said. "*Fuck!* I'm so sorry, dude—oh my god, oh my god. *Fuck, dude.* It was all Sophia's idea! She got it out and showed me!" She moved all over on the couch, antsy as hell.

"*Um!*" I was dumbfounded. I didn't know what to say. *Are you kidding me?* I was racking my brain to make sure this wasn't my fault. That I didn't deserve this for some reason, that I had the right to be mad. "That is a *complete* violation of privacy. No question. That's wrong. That's *so* fucked up!" I felt the urge to apologize for some reason, but I stood my ground.

She got up off the couch. "Okay, well, I have to go because . . . well, I'm going to Jake's but . . . are we gonna be okay?"

"I don't know!" I shouted. I couldn't believe what was happening. "I don't know! Just go!"

Sophia was the one who opened the document on Google Drive. Dance Man had just broken up with her, completely out of the blue. She had been a wreck the previous two weeks. I could see her spinning out of control and it was like looking into a mirror.

"I can't believe this is how you've been feeling," she cried to me one night, a few days after Dance Man dumped her. I wouldn't wish what I felt that semester on my worst enemy, but it was validating to see I wasn't the only train-wreck after a breakup.

Rachel told me Sophia went searching for my diary because she knew there was stuff about me and Yes Man breaking up in there, and she said she was searching for solace. *Fair.* But she searched for her own name within the document. She searched Rachel's name and offered for her to read. Rachel said yes.

I walked into Sophia's room and told her I knew what she did.

"Well, you shared it with me," she said, like it was plain as day and as if I should have seen it coming. I'm not sure how she had access, but in some way she did. I suppose it was a mistake on my end for not understanding how Google Drive works, but *still.* People *read my diary*, and didn't tell me they did, and told a lot of people about it.

I let out a laugh. I couldn't believe her response. "Okay, wow," I breathed out as calmly as I could. "This is my last night here. Sutton is coming over and I'm going to pack. I don't want to see you until I leave." I got up and left the room.

That was the last straw.

There are two types of people in this world: those who read people's diaries and those who don't. For example, my mom has watched my stack of diaries grow, year after year, as she comes in my room to drop off clean laundry. Not *once* has she laid a finger on them. I know this is true.

I needed good, supportive people in my life. I needed people I could trust. I needed people who wouldn't pull shit like this. I vowed then and there to become the friend I needed.

These breakup chapters go out to anyone who is "looking for solace." Heartbreak is the worst feeling, and it's even worse if nobody understands what you're going through. If any of this resonates with you at all, I just want to say: *you're going to be okay. I promise.*

Friends: A How-to Guide in Process

———

December 26, 2020

Age 21, senior year of college

It's never too late to take a hard look at yourself and question if you're really living the life you want to—if you're really being the person you want to be.

I understand that some people are stuck in certain situations. There is always nuance to a bold claim. Recognizing your mistakes and patterns and making a conscious decision to work in a new direction takes courage, humility, and resilience.

It's not fun to look at all the nasty parts of yourself. I don't like it. But I don't want to be stuck with these patterns forever.

I'm done letting who I was in the past dictate how I live my future. I'm done letting people tell me who I am and who I'm not. I'm done having fake confidence that's loud and coming from a place of hurt. I'm done with people that talk shit on other people. I'm done being friends with people that I habitually talk shit on—what's the point of being friends with someone that I just don't like? I'm done being in unfulfilling friendships. I'm done having casual sex with people that I just don't want to. I'm done looking for external validation in places that have shown me that it's not coming. I'm done making excuses for my fear. I'm done saying that I can't do something for some made-up reason. I'm done doubting myself because it's not getting me very far.

I'm done settling for my own behaviors that annoy the shit out of me.

What makes me nervous about writing this book at such a young age is the fear some people will see me as naive, or even worse: a hypocrite. So be it. I'm twenty-one. I'm out here *guessing*. I have no idea if what I say I'm going to do is going to work! I just have to live and find out, and make adjustments as I go. That's all I can do. Oh—there's the "yes, and" again.

The fall semester of my junior year in college was a breaking point. My relationship crumbled to the ground, my two closest friendships went up in flames, and my self-esteem was shot. Everything exploded. I stood in the ashes the morning after I found out about the diary incident, and I vowed to do some serious growing up.

After years of friendships dramatically blowing up in my face, I knew I had to work on cultivating lasting, fulfilling friendships. But it dawned on me I had never had incredibly healthy friendships in the first place. How could I have good friendships if I didn't know what a good friendship even looked like?

I started with myself. After hitting rock bottom, I had no choice but to confront who I was, why things had gone wrong in my relationship and friendships, who I *wanted* to be, and who I wanted to *surround myself with.* I became acutely intentional about the people I chose to spend time with, and went even deeper into improving myself.

Because quite frankly, I was tired of feeling like shit.

I made lists of things I didn't like about myself, which I don't necessarily recommend doing unless you plan on writing positive things afterward. It was humbling to call out bad habits I had in an effort to start recognizing them and take steps to grow out of them. I also made lists of things I loved, which was really fun.

I love jazz, red wine, dancing, wearing jeans and black t-shirts, the *idea* of philosophy but not *actual* philosophy, people with weird habits who aren't ashamed of them, graphic design, my crazy brother, being outside, improv, anything red, drinking games that turn *very* personal, French DJs, architecture, restaurants with cool lighting, being a devil's advocate, Buddhism, podcasts, belly laughs, and writing. Stuff like that.

What you love speaks volumes about who you are. Although it sounds simple, once you lay out what you love, you can actively seek those things out and craft a life full of things you love when it's in your control. I don't have a lot of advice, but if you're searching for a deeper meaning of who you are, try starting with what you love.

I asked myself:

Who do I feel most loved by? Who do I feel safe around?
Who consistently shows up for me, no matter what?

I remembered specific times when I had felt safe and loved and free to express myself around people. I asked what that friend did to make me feel that way. I wrote it down and tried to learn what it means to be a good friend.

Sutton: The Art of Listening

"—and it's all just *so* freaking *annoying*, and I don't know what to do!!!" I wailed over FaceTime with Sutton, weekly, as I melodramatically recounted the saga of the day. When I was finally done and out of breath from yelling, Sutton nodded her head slowly.

"Hmm...." She pondered. "I see . . ."

"Well? What do you think I should do?" I pressed on urgently.

"What do you *want* to do?" she asked.

"What?" I immediately stopped pacing my room, caught off guard.

"What do *you* want to do about it?" she insisted.

"Well. I—I —" I stammered, surprised with the sense of autonomy I forgot I had. "I guess I want to drop the class?" I asked, as if it was a question she had the answer to.

"Okay, then drop it," she said matter-of-factly, never *once* inserting her own opinion. This would happen at least once a week.

Her patience is truly breathtaking. Something I desperately struggle with is sharing my own experience with others when they are asking for advice or venting.

Sutton actually listens. She is comfortable with silence. She doesn't interrupt or interject her own judgments. She takes time to process what I say, and I wait patiently for her response, which is usually just a question to guide me deeper. It's magic.

For my birthday this past year, she framed the coffee bag I designed for Brevé, my dad's business. I called her so many times that year complaining about designing the new bag. I called her so many times when they were finished and I wanted to showcase my hard work. Framing that bag in a sparkling glass case was the ultimate form of listening. It says, "I heard you, and I understand how important this is to you." It's hanging on the wall above the desk in our family's kitchen.

I want to be a better listener like Sutton.

Sage: The Art of Giving

"Kelly, let's go on a trip. Let's get you out of here," Sage said as she pulled out her laptop and started searching for Airbnbs in Newport. I had just told her Yes Man and I broke up. There were no more questions asked. We hopped in the car and got the hell out of Manhattan for a weekend. She didn't ask what I wanted; she just gave me what I needed, and it meant the world.

"Sage, what's all this?" I gasped as I walked into her apartment after a terribly stressful week at work one summer. Her apartment was sparkling clean with fresh flowers and candles and she was cooking steaks on the stove.

"Oh no!" She swatted her hands down at me. "You go sit down. It's been a long week. My treat." I sat down in disbelief and we had a candlelit steak dinner, and Sage let me talk her ear off for hours. The next morning, I woke up to a five-star breakfast in the kitchen. "Eat up before work," she said casually.

I want to be a better giver like Sage.

Norah: The Art of Context

"What are you doing tonight?" Norah texted me one night. It was the fall semester of my junior year and I was just beginning to spiral.

"I think I might hang out with Max, but he hasn't texted me back," I replied.

"Hmm.... Why don't you come over? We can have wine and play guitar and watch a movie. It'll be great." She was right. I went over and we had a wonderful time. I forgot all about Max. She saved me from a night of anxiously checking my phone and putting energy into a useless boy. I confided in her about how lost and lonely I was feeling. I told her about the intervention my roommates had with me and how I was struggling with knowing myself.

"Oh my god...." she said, and her eyes softened. "I had no idea. Thanks for telling me all of this. Now I know to check in and spend more time with you." It was such a transparent thing to say, and a vulnerable thing to receive.

"Thank you.... I think I need that right now," I said sincerely. We took walks every Sunday that semester and she always made sure to send a *how are you* text throughout the week. I felt safe and supported, knowing a friend was thinking of me and my situation even when we weren't together.

I want to hold space for my friends' contexts like Norah.

Irena: The Art of Cheerleading

Irena walked into the restaurant and started walking toward the back where I was sitting. We had a big falling out our senior year of high school because she didn't invite me to her birthday party, and I didn't wish her a happy birthday as revenge. We didn't speak for a year. My heart was beating anxiously. As she got closer, she started to smile, and I noticed tears in her eyes.

"Ah! Kelly!" She outstretched her arms toward me, and I stood up to hug her. She was crying! Happy crying! We sat down and she gave me the biggest smile. "Wow," she breathed out. "Kelly, . . . I took our friendship in high school for granted, and I'm sorry. I've grown up a lot this year and I miss you."

Damn. Irena is the most hardcore, badass young woman anyone has ever met. I was stunned. We had a long conversation about what we had achieved in our first year of college and how excited we were to go back in the fall. She texted me afterward.

"I'm proud to be your friend. You're awesome," the text read. This was revolutionary because Irena and I spent high school one-upping and feeling threatened by one another. One time, she scored higher than me on a chemistry test and I told everyone she cheated. She didn't. I was just insecure.

Throughout college, Irena and I have cheered each other on. I sent her flowers on the day she took the LSAT, and she sent me flowers back in return to celebrate my one-year anniversary of being Single Kelly again. She was the first person to pre-order this book, and she bought one hundred dollars' worth of copies. Our friendship has evolved from comparison and envy to a genuine pride in each other's accomplishments. It's living proof of women supporting women in a world where we are conditioned to feel like another woman's success takes away from our own. It doesn't.

I want to show my friends I'm proud of them like Irena does.

Melanie: The Art of Humor

"You know, sometimes sarcasm is better than therapy," I mused in the car with Melanie as we drove down to the Lake of the Ozarks.

"Ain't that the fuckin' truth!" She laughed and pointed to the Snoop Dogg bobble head on her dashboard that was getting smacked by the hot pink rosary swinging from her rearview mirror. We were eating gas station hot dogs.

I'd love to detail the infinite inside jokes Melanie and I have—the ones that have me laughing on the ground in the fetal position, unable to catch my breath—but you just had to be there. Melanie is one of those friends who you FaceTime and instantly start laughing before either of you has said anything because just their essence is funny.

"What's up?" She answers FaceTime as she wraps her hair around a curling iron.

"Getting ready for a stupid Hinge date," I answer, rubbing bronzer all over my face.

"Ew, me too. I don't even wanna go," she says, painting on her winged eyeliner.

"Me neither. I rather eat pizza and die," I joke, spraying my nicest perfume on my neck just in case.

These days, Melanie and I trek together through the unexplored jungle of online dating and obsess over the minute perils of dating in your early twenties. Having a partner in crime who makes me laugh until I cry makes this chaotic time actually enjoyable. There are friends you call when you want to reflect about your feelings and the universe, and there's friends like Melanie who you call when you want to twerk, take a tequila shot, and eat gas station hot dogs. Amen.

I want to make my friends laugh until they cry more like Melanie.

Aside from everything these people have taught me about friendship, I can also say each of these people inspire me in how they live their own lives. Sutton is honorably humble. Sage stands up for herself. Norah forges her own path shamelessly. Irena pursues her own niche interests and doesn't care what people think about them. Melanie, selflessly and gracefully, takes on a lot of responsibility.

The Bible was really onto something when it told us to treat others how we want to be treated. I think that shit might actually be the answer. As I gear up to take on more of my twenties, I'd like to share with you a few more lessons I have learned along the way that I hope to take with me.

1. Envy and comparison are the thieves of trustworthy companionship. Our own insecurities tear others down. Good friendships start with healthy self-esteem.

2. If you feel compelled to talk badly about someone when they are not in the room, you might need to reevaluate what they bring to the table. Strive to have friends in your life who you can't wait to brag about.

3. There are people who drain your energy and people who elevate your energy. You have a choice in who you spend time with. Choose wisely.

4. Letting go of a friendship that isn't serving you does not make you a bad person, even if it leaves a sour taste in your mouth.

5. Take responsibility when you mess up, and make sure you learn from your own mistakes so you don't keep hurting the same person.

6. Sometimes friends just need you to listen. People don't always need advice; they just need to air shit out and have a safe space to do it in.

7. If someone hurts your feelings, let them know. If you don't say anything, they might repeat that action without knowing it hurts you, and you start to resent them. Trust that good friends don't *want* to hurt you, but sometimes they don't know they did unless you tell them. (Ugh, this is so hard for me!)

8. Try to have realistic expectations of others. You can have different friends for different things. Don't expect the same thing from everyone, because again, everyone brings something different to the table.

9. Strive to understand the context of other people's actions. What are they going through? How can you be of service to them? Read the room: if they're dealing with big family problems, don't complain about having a bad salad for lunch, okay?

10. Boundaries: someone please write a textbook on this topic. Know the behaviors you are willing to accept from people, and put a hard stop on the ones you don't accept. Know when to make sacrifices for a friend. Know when to give yourself space. This will probably take me a lifetime to learn.

This list is just as much for me as it is for whoever is reading this. I still have a lot to learn! All I want is to sit back in my rocking chair—just kidding—my red, velvet chaise lounge when I'm seventy-five and say, "we've been friends for over fifty years!" as I raise a dirty martini to the crowd of loved ones at my seventy-fifth birthday party. That's how I'll know I've made it.

The After-Party:
A Spiritual Cocktail

February 28, 2015

Age 16, sophomore year of high school

"And then what do we live for if not for something next?"

"Live for now." Well, isn't that easier said than done, my friend.

Stephen Hawking, one of the most brilliant minds to grace this earth, practically declared that there is no God.

No God?

How?

Without God, . . . what, in fact, is the reason and purpose for life? Why do we live? On accident? Does that not seem completely and utterly ridiculous to you?

If you just imagine for a second, a life without God, a life without a bigger meaning. . . . Well, I feel that it's quite impossible to decipher. My whole life and upbringing would be a lie. A theory.

Am I wasting my time? I can't really put it into words. I can't fathom it. It's like everything stops. Silence. Except for the slow, insidious ticking of the clock. I can't imagine life being that way. Perhaps I don't have the words to do this thought any justice.

Maybe I'll come back to it in a few years. Until then, I'll be keeping the faith.

I really set myself up there. I guess now would be a good time to revisit this!

As of current, my spirituality is somewhat of a signature cocktail: a Spiritual Cocktail, that is. I am a born and raised Irish Catholic so, of course, there is alcohol involved. The spiritual cocktail is a work in process, but I'll share my recipe so far. Feel free to modify for your own taste.

Ingredients:

- Eighteen years of Catholic Guilt

- That one time I watched *The Theory of Everything* with Eddie Redmayne and journaled about it (see excerpt above)

- One statue of Buddha that sits atop two Buddhist books I did, in fact, read

- The Headspace app

- *The Daily Stoic* book

- A lot of Atheist and Jewish friends

- Motivational speakers on podcasts

- Student-discount therapy

- Saying things like, "the Universe"

- Self-help infographics on Instagram

- A picture of my mom with an orb in the background she claims is my late grandfather's soul

- A splash of whiskey

- Garnish with uncertainty

It's no secret how I grew up; I've made that explicitly clear. I was *really, really* into the Catholic Church. I thought it was so freaking cool we had the Vatican, basilicas, different rankings of priests, and massive golden cathedrals all around the world. I loved the rituals, the rules, the history, and the Bible stories. I loved the idea of not being alone, and having a bigger thing to lift everything up to.

When I was younger, I was much more literal and serious like my mother. I thought it was perfectly clear what was right and wrong. Well, of course it was clear: it was shoved down my throat every day from eight to three, for twelve years. I loved the idea of having a strict moral compass and doing things right. I sat on top of a high horse and looked down on others when I decided they were sinning. I practically invented my own version of cancel culture at age ten.

The very first time I masturbated, I went to school the next morning and searched for the priest. I begged him to do Confession with me. I could hardly live with myself. The Bible said if you did stuff like that, you had to cut off your right hand. I figured it was better to tell an old white guy what I did than to chop my own hand off.

In high school, when I found out my friends started having sex, I immediately deemed them as unholy and weak.

"You really should go to Confession," I'd tell them from atop of my moral high horse. I can't believe I did this. But at the time, indulging in such an act was a sign of weakness! I was holding out! I had willpower! Yes Man, given he said yes to *everything*, even said yes to waiting.

I had a rude awakening in college—or maybe I should call it an Enlightenment. Turns out, the general public has a not-so-flattering opinion of the Catholic Church! During orientation week at WashU, our program organized for us to go watch a film at the Tivoli Theater, a famous theater in St. Louis. We watched *Spotlight*, which is a film about the investigation into a priest who molested more than eighty boys. Apparently, it was a well-known thing to my peers at the time the Catholic Church had this reputation. This was news to me.

Hardly anyone I've met at WashU has been Catholic. WashU has a very vibrant and engaging Jewish community. When Christmas came around, there were no Christmas trees, but posters for Hanukkah. When Easter came around, classes weren't cancelled for Holy Thursday and Good Friday; there were announcements for Passover and my friends hosted Seders. My friends loved going to Jewish holiday gatherings. Their holidays sounded fun and cool!

They all came back and talked about how they drank wine and talked and ate great food!

It is a very tight-knit community from what I've experienced, and everyone seems to take pride in their faith. Meanwhile, I have felt a bit embarrassed in college about being raised Catholic. I suppose I could have engaged more with the Catholic Student Center at WashU, but so much of me wanted a break from rules being shoved down my throat.

One night in my freshman year dorm room, a group of girls came over and we all started chatting. A few girls were sharing riveting sexual experiences and pumping each other up, saying stuff like, *"yes!* Get it, girl, that's what you *need!"* They talked so freely and openly about sex. They started talking about masturbating and how much they loved their vibrators. They talked about the importance of sex education and female liberation from the patriarchy or something. I sat on my bed with wide, curious eyes. I knew boys talked about this stuff all the time, but I didn't realize we could too.

I thought talking about sex was underground and taboo at the time. Although a bit uncomfortable, it was exciting to see people shamelessly embrace something I had always wanted to, but felt a deep sense of guilt and shame around—as I'm sure anyone raised very religiously can attest to. But the conversation felt so right to me, and I questioned whether my form of sex education was more harmful than helpful.

After being exposed to new ways of thinking—and resenting my upbringing for making me feel stupid—I became very defiant of all things Catholicism. I felt like

I had been lied to for eighteen years, and I wanted some time to go out and explore some other options.

I've scraped the surface of a few more religions. I've talked to Sikh friends, my Mormon neighbors, Jewish friends, and people who are Christian but not necessarily Catholic. I read Herman Hesse's *Siddhartha*, and it changed my life. I read another Buddhist book by Dr. Tara Brach called *Radical Acceptance* that employed a lot of Buddhist teachings. I aligned so much with them! I meditate sometimes and find that to be much more spiritual than Mass. And I think to myself, *who's right? Who's wrong? What if they're all right? What if they're all wrong? What if Stephen Hawking was right?*

On one of my many dates in New York, a guy asked me very bluntly and out of nowhere if I believed in God. I felt like he was asking *just to check*. It felt like he was *making sure*. It had the same tone of someone saying, "You're not a psychopath, are you? 'Kay, didn't think so.'" I was so caught off guard.

"Do *you*?" I asked, not sure how to answer this question for the first time in my life. I noticed I didn't have an answer to his question.

"Fuck no. That shit's ridiculous." He took a sip of wine. He was kind of a douche, but he paid for a hell of a nice meal. I felt like an idiot. *Was I ridiculous?* Most of the guys I've casually dated after Yes Man have all voiced their staunch Atheism. It makes me uncomfortable. Ironically, the two Catholic guys I've been out with both wore crosses around their neck and that made me uncomfortable too. Seeing other people be so certain makes me uncomfortable because I am not certain about anything—hence the cocktail.

WashU, being the progressive and forward-thinking sphere it is, is home to a lot of Atheists. Perhaps they are right. I'm sure they are. *Good for them*, I say! *You have the answers! You can die a very boring death and not worry about it!* But hanging out with these people makes me embarrassed to admit I went to Catholic school my entire life. I feel like it makes me look silly, or it makes my parents look crazy.

"I would never send my kids to a religious school; it's kinda fucked up," people have said to me, and I wonder if *I'm* fucked up. I went out of my way not to do much with the Catholic community at WashU, which is why I experienced having *no one* to relate to on topics like this. In college, it has seemed like everyone is on the same page about either being Jewish or Atheist, and I have missed the memo.

I think I do need something more though, especially given the already fantastical and unrealistic view I have of the physical realm. An afterlife sounds like a very cool after-party I wouldn't want to miss—even if it's just *hope* of an after-party.

I've done a complete one-eighty with my perspective. Where I was once a believer in strict adherence to The Ten Commandments, I am much more open-minded and welcoming of new ideas. In fact, I am fascinated by new ideas and I want to ascribe to them all—even Atheism sometimes! You know, now that I think about it, my horoscope did tell me I could be susceptible to joining a cult. So maybe that's what it is. The point is that in a perfect world, everyone could freely, openly, and shamelessly embrace their own beliefs, so long as it doesn't cause any hardships. Other than that, carry on, I say!

In 2020, I had an opportunity to revisit Catholicism a bit. After being yanked back home to Imperial, Missouri to live with my parents again for an indefinite time—insert: Covid-19—I had the space to revisit my roots.

In April 2020, my family put our two dogs, Kemper and Libby, down. Those dogs grew up with me for fourteen years. They had seen it all. Putting them down wasn't as hard as I thought it would be, but I found myself believing, or *hoping*, their souls—or whatever they are—are somewhere out there in the Universe. I don't know the specifics; I'll get back to you on that never.

In August 2020, my grandpa passed away. It was my first grandparent to pass, and the closest person I've lost. He was a devout Catholic man. He worked and paid for his own high school tuition because he was so set on going to a Catholic high school. This was my mom's dad, and he was just as literal and serious as she is. He would say things like, "religion is just to control the masses, you know," but still went to Mass every Sunday. This always confused me. But now I'm wondering if he chose to have faith anyway, regardless of the facts.

We had a wonderful Catholic Mass for the funeral. It was really cool to see our forty-plus members' extended family all bow their heads and pray together. Some people might argue all religion does is make people feel better about death and offer them closure. If that's all religion is good for, so be it. I'm still not sure of what I believe right now, but sharing in those rituals and the sacrament was really important to me.

During those spring and summer months of Covid-19, I found myself returning a bit of my attention to spirituality. When I'm feeling anxious, as most of us felt during 2020, I find myself reflexively saying Hail Marys in my head to calm me down. There's something cathartic about lifting your worries up to something bigger and greater than yourself.

Going through my old diary entries has reminded me of what a big influence religion has played in my upbringing. Though I'll admit some things could have been taught in a different light, I think right now I'm feeling pretty grateful to have grown up with some sort of structure. And even if it's not Catholicism that does it for me, at least I've been exposed to religion and know that's an option if I ever decide to have another identity crisis and want to do the Born-Again-Christian thing. I'll let you know.

All in all, I think right now I'll be sipping my spiritual cocktail I've so creatively shaken up. A little bit of Buddha, some Irish Whiskey, and a dash of Hawking to make things interesting. I encourage you to make your cocktail however you'd like. Maybe I'll see you at the after-party, maybe I won't. Either way, I think we're all just trying to have a good-ass time. Cheers.

A Truly Irish Goodbye

You know how people going through an identity crisis say stuff like, "Oh, I need to go find myself," and indulge in some traveling—looking for themselves in museums and hiking trails and French lovers?

I did that, minus the French lover part. I wish. Though I wanted to study abroad in Singapore, the Universe smelled the God and whiskey in my blood and sent me to Ireland. I have no complaints, other than the fact there are no food preservatives and the grocery store was a forty-five-minute bus ride away. This resulted in me, a four-foot-eleven-inch and one-hundred-pound thing, eating an entire bag of brussel sprouts and two chicken breasts for dinner because I knew they were going bad the next day, and I didn't know when I'd make it back to the store. I gained ten pounds in two months. But alas, it was the best two months of my life.

The airport bus dropped me off at a stop about a half mile outside of University College Dublin. I stood alone in the cold January rain with two fifty-pound suitcases and not a clue where I was going. I started walking, one foot in front of the other, dragging my baggage behind me, squinting through the rain and tensing my shoulders from the cold.

I finally made it, after several wrong turns, to my apartment for the semester. It was tiny and wonderful and overlooked a patch of the greenest grass I had ever seen. My roommates were strangers and I couldn't have been happier. I had no obligation to them, and it was liberating—as opposed to my previous fall semester at WashU. That tiny shoe box of a room felt more like home for the two and half months I was there than my room at WashU the previous fall had. The isolation forced me to be alone and confront the explosions and ashes from the past year.

I think what people mean when they say they want to find themselves through traveling is they want to be taken out of their contexts. Going to Europe felt like a claw machine picked me up out of a ditch, swung me overseas, and plopped me up onto the ground somewhere completely different and finally safe. I couldn't have gone at a better time.

There were a lot of WashU kids who came to University College Dublin, or UCD. Originally, it was only supposed to be two other kids and me but the Hong Kong abroad program was cancelled due to the ongoing protests in 2020. So the twenty-something kids who wanted to travel Asia and experience *real* culture shock were told they were going to Dublin. This was great news to me! Now I had connections!

The WashU kids I met in Ireland are some of the best WashU people I have met throughout my entire college experience. It was a random group of kids. Most of them I had never met; they were computer science and finance majors so that explains why our paths never crossed. But they were incredible.

"Kelly, some of us are hiking on Saturday. Do you want to come?" My friend Daniel asked as we walked back to campus from the bus stop. An invitation! I was so flattered! I barely knew Daniel at the time!

"Of course! I'll be there!" I promised with a happy smile. Flash forward twenty-four hours later, and I was trudging through rocks and mud and realizing Doc Martens and jeans are not hiking attire. I wound up getting discounted hiking boots for my twenty-first birthday—something I never expected to want.

We hiked all the way to the tip of Sugarloaf Mountain in County Wicklow. When we got to the top of the mountain, we unpacked the groceries we packed and made sandwiches. Freezing wind swirled around us and we squinted our eyes from the sun beating down on us. We shivered and huddled together as we passed bread, ham, and mustard down the line of us sitting on top of rocks overlooking the Irish Sea, green pastures dotted with white sheep, and Dublin in the distance. It was one of the coolest moments of my life. Mostly just because it was one of the first times I had organized a big excursion without my parents.

"This reminds me of a mountain I hiked in Spain," Daniel mused as he took a bite of his sandwich.

"Yeah!" Our friend Marc from Australia joined in. "The climb up was like the mountain marathons I do back home. They last three days long, and we camp as we go!"

"Oh no way! That's sick!" My friend Ethan perked up. "I usually wind up backpacking and camping when I go on rock climbing trips."

"Oh, you climb?" Lexie cheered. "Me too! Let's find a place to climb next week!"

I had nothing to add. My hobbies consisted of improv and writing and wanting to live in a big city and wear fancy clothes.

As I sat on top of that mountain, wind whipping my face and mayonnaise freezing on my lips, a new dimension of aspirations appeared. Suddenly, I was questioning the excitement of the busy cosmopolitan lifestyle. I was intrigued by a new set of challenges: the great outdoors! I hadn't embarked on any of the adventures these new friends had. I never even thought about stuff like backpacking, and it all sounded very cool, exciting, and fulfilling.

I have never been camping, never been backpacking—hell, that was my first *real* hike. Climbing up that mountain on my hands and knees on the steep rocks, looking down to see how far I would fall if I slipped, was an entirely new brand of exhilarating.

We walked fourteen miles, took a few buses, and finally made it back to campus. Then, we all decided to go out to nightclubs in Dublin. These people wanted to *do more*! I was so happy! I always find myself wanting to do more, but it's hard to find people who keep up!

Ah. Going out in Dublin may be the closest I ever get to partying like state college kids. I felt so fucking free. It was fantastic. At night, Dublin's windy, black cobblestone streets twinkled from string lights above. Every close-knit building was painted a bright red, green, or yellow and had undeniable history and character. It was always loud at night with people singing in the streets and dancing in pubs. Everyone slammed together pints of Guinness in rowdy toasts. The chaos felt like home.

I finally had my nights of taking shots, dancing, laughing until I cried, making out with random Irish guys, bumming cigarettes off of strangers, pretending to be European, eating McDonald's at three in the morning, and not remembering how I got back to my apartment when I woke up at noon the next day. It was paradise.

Though it wasn't some silent meditation retreat, those late nights out sure felt like a spiritually healing experience to me. When I'm forty-five, I don't think drinking vodka straight out of a flask I keep in my purse will be an acceptable method of catharsis, but I was twenty-one, so screw it. I had fun, and it was just like the movies! Finally!

January 30, 2020

23 minutes before my 21st birthday

> *In 23 minutes, I turn 21. You know, I always imagined what 21 would look like and feel like. Never in a million years would I have expected that I'd be sitting in a tiny shoebox of a room in Dublin, Ireland with amazing people that I hadn't even met a month ago.*

> *I didn't expect to wash my face and see this person staring back at me in the mirror. She's not who I thought she'd be. She's better—much cooler too. I definitely thought I*

would be taller though. I didn't expect to have so many earrings, and I most certainly didn't think that I'd have a tiny tattoo on my arm that says, "yes, and".

I kind of thought I would be a cheerleader at Alabama but alas, I'm a junior at WashU, which is a very different place. I didn't think I would question my Catholic upbringing as much as I do. But I knew I would be the person to change my major a lot, which I have, and still might do again. Fashion to architecture to graphic design to marketing to economics and back to marketing. I guess I've become sort of a risk-taker, which I'm proud of and hope to continue.

I didn't think I'd be on a college improv team. Okay, well, maybe I did, but I didn't think I'd perform in front of 300 kids and be recognized on campus by strangers. I didn't think I would go to college with my high school sweetheart, and I really didn't think we were going to break up this summer. It's kind of beautiful to have fallen in love at sixteen and have my heart broken at twenty—I'm okay with that. I've learned more about myself through this breakup than anything else.

I didn't think I'd be the type of person to ever question marriage or even my sexuality for that matter, but all of a sudden, I have the freedom to do that. I didn't think I'd be a solo-adventurer, Eat Pray Love kind of person. I'm still not, but I want to be, which is new.

"In The Mood" by Glenn Miller is still my favorite song. I still come home from parties and put headphones in so I can keep dancing in my room. I love dancing. I always will. I didn't think I'd ever like The Grateful Dead because the name sounds like scary screamo music, but turns out I really love it and it's not scary at all—it's actually very groovy! (Did I just say that? Whatever!) Am I one of those

kinds of people now? Those people that wear tie dye and bandanas? I guess we'll see.

I definitely thought I would be more of a Charlotte York, but I've switched my pearls for hoops. Speaking of which, I didn't think I would have had a summer in New York City under my belt by this point in my life. It always seemed like such a fantasy to live in the big city, but I have! And I worked for freaking NBC, are you kidding?

Oh! It's 12:00. Well, cheers to you, kid. Damn. Just like that. Twenty-one is old enough to look back and recognize different versions of myself, and young enough to still make a thousand decisions about who I want to become. Oh! There's the "yes, and" again.

"Kelly! What should we do for your birthday?" My friend Jill asked me one day as we drank coffee at a bookstore in Dublin. My birthday was still a week away, and I was shocked people cared. Maybe they just wanted an excuse for something to do, or maybe they actually liked me! Imagine that!

"Oh! Yeah!" I smiled ear-to-ear. "You know . . . I just wanna go to a cool restaurant and dance all night."

I turned twenty-one only a few weeks after arriving in Dublin. I was really nervous because I was celebrating a pretty big birthday with friends I had just met. I was worried it would be awkward. But no. We went to a cool restaurant and danced all night! My twenty-first birthday was perhaps the best birthday I've had.

Everyone seemed excited to be there! People bought me shots at dinner and took my picture and sang "Happy

Birthday!" It seems so trivial, but damn. . . . It felt so nice to have people around me who seemed to *want* to be there with me, to not have Yes Man baggage, to not have roommate baggage. These people only knew me as Kelly. They didn't know Yes Man and Kelly. They didn't know about my obnoxious breakup shenanigans or hear about what my roommates discovered in my diary. They just knew *me* in the context of *me*, and it felt so damn good. *That* was healing.

I remember texting Sutton I finally felt like me again, and I was around people who made me feel comfortable to celebrate being in my own skin. I felt very lucky. I still do.

"Let's go to Vienna next weekend," Jill said in the library at UCD, turning her computer around to show me how cheap the airfare was.

"That's in Austria, right?" She smiled and nodded. "Okay," I said, realizing I was kind of a grown up and I didn't have to ask my parent's permission. And off we went!

My mouth hung open as we walked on the perfectly white cobblestones of Vienna. I was in awe. I felt like I was in a sleepy, whimsical fairy tale. I let out excited squeals any time we so much as passed a building with a decorated railing. I'll never forget walking through Vienna for the first time, hanging onto my backpack and giggling with Jill. I felt so independent. I couldn't believe I had just up and gone to Austria without my parents and with a really cool girl I had met only a few weeks earlier!

The next weekend, I went to Budapest with Drew and Mickey who were on K.A.R.L. with me. Drew and I flew

from Dublin together and Mickey flew from his program in Spain and met us. The three of us shared an Airbnb in the heart of Budapest. We went to the famous ruin bars, baths, and ate amazing, cheap food. One night, we went to an EDM dance club, and I went off the rails. I was front in center of the DJ and jumping up and down, screaming with my eyes closed as the blue strobe lights danced across our faces—in Budapest.

There's no way I even knew what or where Budapest was when I was writing in my cute little diary at age twelve. It just goes to show life will gladly take you to unexpected places if you let it. I didn't even want to go abroad when I was dating Yes Man. Ha! But my utopia came to an abrupt end at 4:33 a.m. on March 12, 2020.

March 21, 2020

Age 21, Imperial, MO

Do I really need to explain it again? I guess. Just in case I decide to publish these diaries one day, or at least let my grandchildren read them, and people want a primary source from someone who lived through Covid-19. Jesus Christ. Okay, here we go.

It was 4:33 am when Lizzy woke me up in the Airbnb I booked for myself in Le Marais.

"Kelly," she said. "We need to leave. Trump just issued a travel ban on Europe. Call your parents, like right now."

"Oh. Okay." I got up and walked across the creaky hard-wood floors, still slightly drunk having only gone to bed a mere hour and a half earlier, and checked my phone.

Three missed calls from Mom. I sighed. I wasn't surprised.
We should have all seen this coming. I mean, I kind of did.
I just didn't want to believe it and I didn't think it would
happen so quickly.

I called my mom and she answered right away.

"Um, hi. You need to book a flight back to St. Louis. Right
now. I can't do it—the Delta website keeps crashing and I
can't call them; it's insane. If you see a flight, book it. Just
get your ass home!"

I got my laptop out and booked a flight for 10:20 a.m. Lizzy
was in the kitchen fighting with her parents on the phone.
I could hear her mom yelling through the phone. My mom
was yelling too. It was the weirdest few minutes of my life
in that tiny studio apartment in Paris in the middle of the
night with international breaking news springing us up
out of our drunken slumber and into a new, unfathomable
reality that ceases to have answers.

Even now as I write this, I have no answers to perhaps one
of the most unprecedented events of the last century? As
of now, 13,608 people have died globally, but I'm sure that
number actually is higher, and will only increase.

"Okay, I booked a flight home," I said, surprised by how
calm my voice sounded. "I'll be in St. Louis at five your
time." I couldn't help but smile a little at the thought of
seeing my mom in a matter of hours.

"Okay. I'll see you then," I heard the smile in her voice.
"You got this."

Lizzy and I hugged and laughed hysterically, or maybe
we just were hysterical. She ran out the door to catch her
train back to her host family. She explained to me what
train to take to get to the airport. I had to leave right

away if I wanted to make my flight. She left, and the door to the apartment shut. I was all alone and somehow had to get myself from Paris to St. Louis. Alone. In the middle of a pandemic.

I took a quick shower, just in case I had to quarantine at a French army base somewhere, and then packed up everything into my backpack. I left the rest of my stuff in Dublin, in my tiny shoebox room at UCD. I put on my black wool coat, tied the straps around my waist, slicked my hair back into a ponytail, and slung my backpack over my shoulders. I walked out of the apartment, down the spiral staircase, through the massive wooden doors, and onto the Parisian streets. It was now 5:23 a.m.

The streets were desolate with a few drunks from the night before and a few café owners setting up for the morning. I walked alone in the dark to the train station. Everything was in French. I wasn't totally sure where I was going. But I figured it out.

It was an hour train ride to the airport. People on the train were wearing face masks. I got to the airport and just started following people up escalators. I had no idea where I was going. Hundreds of Americans were in long, winding lines, on their phones with loved ones, wondering how they were going to get back. After lots of lines, trams, wrong lines, backtracking, and more lines, I made it to my gate.

My seat was in the very last row on the plane. I walked what felt like five city blocks down that plane. But at least I had an aisle seat. It was, ironically, the best flight I've ever been on. I was so comfortable. I was so calm. I think I was just relieved to have gotten a flight, and I was excited to see my family—I really was. That or my fight or flight response had just shut off—I don't know. Even though I had only slept an hour and a half, my eyes were wide open for the entirety of that eleven-hour flight.

The previous couple of weeks were hardly bearable with all the news and fear and uncertainty. I was only in Paris for 36 hours, but every meal I had was spent talking and worrying about Coronavirus. The jokes weren't funny. I told my friend Marc I was probably just going to go home so I wouldn't have to worry. Ha!! I thought I had a choice! What luxury! Choice!

Transferring from Minneapolis to my flight to STL was stressful. I had to go through customs and security. On my way to security, a border patrol officer stopped me.

"Miss, where's your luggage?" I was in a hurry; my flight had started boarding ten minutes earlier.

"I don't have any," I said, out of breath, sweating and hauling ass. I had left everything in Dublin. I just had my backpack on me.

"Miss," he motioned to stop me. "Are you alright?" He looked so concerned that I became concerned. Was I alright? I didn't know! I had to go!

"I flew from Paris. I have to go home. I haven't slept— sorry," I muttered as I walked away.

Another border patrol officer stopped me. I had totally passed up another check point. I showed him my passport quickly and then power walked away.

I was the last person to board the flight to St. Louis. The flight was an hour long. It went by quickly. We landed. Normally when I land back in St. Louis, I have these sentimental moments where I pretend I'm in a movie.

This was different. I didn't feel anything.

I came home from abroad halfway through the semester, without saying goodbye to any of the wonderful friends I had made. I was yanked back, just when I thought I had caught a break.

I got off the plane and called my mom. We were so matter-of-fact about finding each other. Our eyes finally locked and we walked up to each other and then my mom stopped abruptly, a few feet away.

"Can we hug?" I asked, confused.

"I don't know," she said. And then she handed me a medical mask to put on.

"Are you serious?" I asked in disbelief. Was this really happening? It felt so dystopian.

"I mean, yeah, we don't know what this is! You could kill me!" she said. I put it on and then we nervously hugged quickly. I thought that when I got in the car, I would break down and cry from all the overwhelm.

I still haven't cried. It's been nine days.

I've been at home this whole time. I have no idea how long I'll be at home. At least I'll probably have a job in New York for the summer and can leave again in May. There's no way I can stay in Imperial long. Fuck. We have no idea how long this Coronavirus stuff will last.

So I guess I'm quarantining indefinitely. Who knows?

I'm lucky to have hobbies. I've been playing piano and reading a great memoir. I designed a dress. I sketched. This is probably the right time for me to compile all of these diaries and create a memoir or something, but I don't know where to start.

Well, anyway, I'm feeling grateful for having gone abroad. It brought me back to life. It brought me back to Kelly.

My Favorite Day of the Year.

The following entries are excerpts from my diaries on every April 23, a self-proclaimed holiday I created for myself for absolutely no reason.

April 23, 2012

Age 13, seventh grade

> *Wow! The first time I wrote in here was like almost a year ago. I was talking about Connor! Wow, I was such a loser! I'm so more mature now than I was a year ago! By the way, I'm 13 now and in 7th grade. It sucks. I have Mrs. Gray and she stutters like a mother trucker. But at least I have Miss Ko!*

April 23, 2013

Age 14, eighth grade

Hello! Life is great right now! I'm in my last days at St. Joe. I think I have 25 more days? Well, I'm sad to leave Miss Ko, but other than that, I am ready to leave that trap in the dust, even though I have some of my best memories there.

Anyway . . .

I think I went on my first date? So, as you know, me and Josh hang out like every weekend now. It's cool cause we're like best friends. About two weeks ago, he picked me up at my house and we went to the movies. Then we went out to eat and we sat at a table by ourselves! Oh! And he paid for all of it! If that's not a date, then I don't know what is?!

But we're just friends, I think.

Josh came over last night. We were sitting on the red couch and he said something funny. So I laughed and farted!

How fucking embarrassing!

Luckily, we both busted out laughing. He hugged me and said he loved me. Hm. . . . Probably the most embarrassing moment of my life. . . .

April 23, 2014

Age 15, freshman year of high school

My favorite date. April 23rd. Don't ask me why. I just like the sound of it, I guess. So today on April 23, 2014, I woke up, went to school, and had a great time. It was one of those days where I'm happy, hyper, and will talk to anyone.

Those are the best days for me. To me, nothing is better than being comfortable in your own skin and satisfied and content with your life. I'm drama-free! I just go with the flow and enjoy the little things in life. When something goes wrong, I pray, talk to Sabrina, Kristen, Carolyn, or whoever else, then I troubleshoot and think about how to solve my problem.

But what I have found to be remarkably true is to go with your gut: say what you want, and say how you feel. It's scary as hell, and right after you say it, it feels like you've jumped off a cliff and you don't know where you're gonna land. It's always a huge relief when I let something off my chest. "I could never say that to her" is always the excuse, but I can! It generally feels pretty amazing to be honest with someone. So say what you want. Jump off that cliff and land somewhere fantastic! If I'm wrong though, and you somehow land in hell, I'm sorry, but everything happens for a reason.

I love to tell stories. I'm a big storyteller. I wish I had one hundred million stories to tell. That's why I jump off cliffs: to tell the story later. What do I mean when I say jump off cliffs? I mean, sometimes you got to muster up the courage to see what opportunities lie ahead of you. If you don't, you'll be stuck. So I try to take every opportunity that comes my way. . . . Whatever happens out of it, it will just be a good story to tell. And I call it jumping off cliffs because once you do jump, you feel like you've leaped into oblivion, and there's a deep part within each of us that fears oblivion. When you say yes to something or say something to someone that you've been so scared to say, you're jumping. You don't know where you'll land. It's hard to explain. The bottom line is,

1. *Always say how you feel.*
2. *Say yes.*
3. *Jump off cliffs.*
4. *Tell people about all the cliffs that you've jumped off of.*
5. *Enjoy the little things in life. Wait for the little moments that mean a lot.*

So those are my thoughts today on April 23rd, 2014, my favorite day of the year, for no reason. Oh, and laugh a lot!

April 23, 2016

Age 17, junior year of high school

It's nearly one in the morning, but screw it, it's still my favorite day of the year.

Coincidentally, my great-great-grandmother, Mary Josephine Healy—the one who played the piano opening night at Union Station—was married on April 23. I found the marriage license at grandma's house when I was doing my history project. Anyway, now more than ever I want to get married on that day, which is today. I've wanted to get married on this day for no reason at all, other than the fact that it sounds nice when you say it out loud, and "4/23" might look nice engraved onto things like silver picture frames.

It's a Saturday this year, and it'll be a Saturday six years from now, so maybe six years from today, at this time, I'll be getting married to the person I will spend the rest of my life with! Maybe it will be me and Yes Man! We're on the phone right now actually, but he's asleep as usual. We have joked around about it. It's not completely out of the question, really. If we make it through college— that's five years—we could then get engaged, get jobs, get married, and get on with life. It's possible. Unlikely, maybe, but possible? Yes.

Tonight, we talked about what kind of ring I wanted. We were talking about someone else's ring first, though, so don't worry.

"You can design it with my dad. That's what he did for my mom, so that's what you'll do," I said confidently.

"You got this all planned out," he said, looking at me with raised eyebrows from the driver's seat on Manchester, on his way to get ice cream. Hmm. Of course I had it planned out; would you expect anything less?

I love him so much. I do—even all the bad things, I love. Like how he falls asleep in two seconds and I just listen to his heavy breathing on the phone, or even when I talk about something for five minutes and it's not until the last 30 seconds that he decides to start paying attention, or how reluctant he is to even attempt to be on time to anything. He's so calm all the time. This week was the first time he's ever admitted to having a bad day, but he said he was fine. As always. He always says he's fine and okay. It's very contrary to my neurotic outbreaks, tangents, and tantrums that he's been exposed to. That's where we're very different. I'm spastically out of my mind and he's always soothing and calming me down, staying grounded, and being the anchor: something I desperately need, even if it's annoying.

He cut off all of his hair. Wow. If I thought he was cute before, well damn! He's sexy now, let me just tell you. God, even his skin is just so freaking soft and smooth and tan. Wow. I'm just so in love! Sorry! Our six months is next weekend; so long, but so short. I feel like it's been six years and six minutes at the same time. I know you want to hear about me going to New York, and I will get to that soon. I promise! But it's two in the morning, and I've had a long week. So good night, and happy April 23rd!

April 23, 2017

Age 18, senior year of high school

Here it is again: my favorite day of the year. Yes Man decided to go to WashU today. I think I'm still processing how ecstatic I am. Subconsciously, I knew he would go, but that was incredibly stressful waiting for so long to find out—waiting for his family to talk about it, waiting for them to make a decision.

Four more years together! Meeting new people together, going to parties, going to his soccer games, stressing about work together, going over to each other's dorms when we just need to see each other for a second. It's going to be crazy. I hope our relationship continues on its trajectory because I'll marry the hell out of him in a heartbeat! Everything is falling perfectly together. I'm so in love with him. Wow, I really am. He's the most amazing person I know. He really is.

Nine more days of high school left. It's so crazy. It doesn't feel like it's almost over. But it is. I'll never be in high school again. The proms, graduations, and parties will be fun. I'm so excited for it all. I'm so excited to have my family and Yes Man with me. My heart is full and I give it all up to God. I am forever grateful for this life. Forgive me if I do not love it enough. I truly am the most blessed person on earth, and I hope to never take it for granted.

April 23, 2018

Age 19, freshman year of college

Well, you can certainly tell it's been a rough semester by the frequency of my entries. That's good. I need to go through some rough patches every once in a while. New perspectives are positive and progressive, if I dare generalize.

There are a few things on my mind on this night, April 23, 2018:

1. *Yes Man*
2. *Happiness versus fulfillment*
3. *Who am I?*

Wow, typical college ordeals.

Yes Man is pledging his fraternity. He is—surprise, surprise—pledge class president. I'm very proud. He's undoubtably a natural born leader. Watching him get through this tough time reaffirms my choice to love him every day indefinitely. Our relationship sure is taking a toll with him pledging, but also with me being in architecture, K.A.R.L., and Delta Gamma. But this pledging is crazy. He is a slave. I had a date party Friday, and he showed up right before the bus left, and was on his phone the whole dance because he had to be. There was an older member of his frat watching his every move. While we were at the dance and Yes Man was on his phone, this older guy looked over at me and yelled over the music, "get used to him ignoring you! This is his life now!" What a dick. This same guy grabbed Yes Man by the shoulder as soon as the bus back to campus stopped, and shuffled him back to the frat house. I didn't even get to say goodbye.

I went back to my room and drunkenly sobbed and then passed out on the floor. I woke up and then sat on my shower floor and cried some more. He snuck away from the house and came to my room at two a.m. He hugged me so tight for like five minutes. He lay on my bed and started crying. It was terrible. He has no time for anything besides this frat. He has no time for me. I barely have time for him. We're both going through hard times and can't 100 percent be there for each other. We have to find other outlets.

For him, that's his fraternity brothers. For me, it's a little bit trickier. DG hasn't really kicked off yet since we aren't initiated yet. My pledge class doesn't really bond. I'm still only friends with the people I was already friends with before. I also have K.A.R.L., which I have not fully taken advantage of because I spend every waking minute in the architecture studio.

I also realized that I don't even know the last time I had a real best friend besides Yes Man.

He's my rock. The idea of having to replace that is scary. I don't want to break down and be vulnerable in front of people here. I don't want to be a burden on people and take up their time. I'm fine with being open and discussing my life, but I don't have anyone that can just hug me while I cry. Lately, I've been falling apart. Now's the time for me to learn how to be my own glue to put myself together. That's a good lesson to learn. I guess it's what I would learn if we broke up. So now I get to do that without actually having to. That's positive, but it's also scary. It's raising all these questions about my character.

Am I codependent?

Am I more comfortable alone or around people?

Is this a real panic attack or am I forcing this anxiety?

Am I resilient?

Am I strong enough?

*Even though I like architecture and feel fulfilled, am I happy?
Is happiness separate from fulfilment? From success?*

Which am I seeking: happiness or fulfilment?

*Should I switch to boring Arts and Sciences and be happy?
Or stay in architecture and be miserable?*

Can I take care of myself?

Who can I rely on besides Yes Man?

Is it bad that I don't have the answer to that?

*As long as I'm asking questions, I'll inevitably find the
answers. Again, wish me luck.*

April 23, 2019

Age 20, sophomore year of college

*Well, another semester almost down. Another April 23. I
have two exams left and then I'm halfway through college.
Wild. . . .*

*I'm not sure if I can sum up the semester right now. How
was it? Well, it was a lot of things.*

Good: Overall, I am alive and breathing.

Bad: I hate the winter.

Terrible: I found out Yes Man does a lot of coke and lies about it to me. I fucking hate being lied to.

Scary: I went to therapy for the first time for anxiety. One night, I couldn't sleep because my heart would not stop racing. It was all over Yes Man—and school a little, but mostly Yes Man. And I couldn't even admit that in the session, so it was pretty useless.

Sad: I'm putting my dogs down soon, and I recently just found out Grandpa Don has cancer. It's okay, though. He's not the same. He's unhappy, which is sad. My dogs look unhappy too.

Depressing: I had all 8:30 a.m.'s again. I couldn't go to the frat house at nights and hang out with all my friends because I had to wake up, which was so hard because the weather here fucking sucks ass and it's cold and gray and raining and the world hurts your face when you walk outside. But now it's beautiful again!

Fulfilling: Turns out I really like Communication Design and wound up having a good time with the last couple projects.

Exciting: I flew to NYC over spring break and interviewed for Late Night with Seth Meyers! I didn't get it. But I am working for NBC this summer at 30 Rock, with Syfy, doing Creative Marketing and Production. I know. Sorry to drop this bomb so casually because it's not casual at all! But I have been so busy! I don't even know how much longer I should write this because I have to wake up early and study.

Eye-opening: My friends are really rich and I am not and it makes me sad. I have thought a lot about money this semester. My dad finally sat me down and went over my *student loans with me. I just owe for the one semester of WashU that wasn't covered by my mom's work, and room and board. Literally one semester and room and board at WashU is worth taking out loans for. I didn't realize how much I'm going to owe once I graduate, and it was overwhelming. It's $687 a month for six or seven years. That's a lot. And none of my friends, at least that I know of, have to worry about that, which is unfair to say because maybe they do, but I feel really resentful of wealthy kids at this school whose parents pay for them to just do drugs, sleep in, and skip class. How could you ever skip class at a school like this?!*

Fun: I went to Wine and Cheese at Sig Nu a few weeks ago after a K.A.R.L. show and was dancing with all my DG friends and just started cracking up because I was like yay! College is so fun and I love dancing! And I've had many nights like this!

Weird: My roommate is really struggling. She's going to a rehab center in Utah this summer for bulimia, bipolar, and alcoholism. There's puke in the carpet outside of my suite that has never been cleaned up. I step in it every day. There were many nights I would come home to her screaming very alarming things, and I would have to call an RA or someone to help. I think my roommate hates me for getting involved, but things like mental health at this severity are out of my control. I hope she gets better. She has the kindest soul. I miss her. Watching her deteriorate has been so horrible and sad to watch.

Uncomfortable: I found out in NYC that Yes Man trips acid. And lies to me about it. Go figure. Before this, I had considered breaking up with him: hence the major anxiety. We had a pretty rough time this semester and I cried a lot. I think it was literally just because I missed him and he was busy and he's bad at answering his phone so I thought he didn't like me? He likes me though. I just was freaking out for like three months. I think it's fine now? Our three and a half year anniversary is next week.

Exciting: Did I mention I'm working at 30 Rock this summer?

Rewarding: I like the work I produced this semester.

Reflective: I feel this one all the time. I'm always self-aware— always wondering how I can be better.

April 23, 2020

Age 21, junior year of college

This day again.

I hereby release this date from being my wedding day. In fact, it should probably be anything but that.

How am I doing this year?

Honestly, I don't know.

We are in the midst of a global pandemic. I had to come home from abroad. I barely do school. I have no romantic life. I work out every day. I eat well, and I'm not stressed. I'm helping Brevé a lot. We're losing a lot of money because of Covid-19. It's all very unexpected.

Most days, I enjoy myself. Other days, I feel depressed and can hardly move. I FaceTime some good friends. I spend too much time on dating apps, scrolling and making disgusted faces. I hate dating apps. I'm probably not going to have a job this summer. I'll probably work for my dad. So things are good but very, very weird. I feel like I'm fifteen again. Hardly any school, no stress, no boyfriend. I only have me to focus on, which is probably good in the long run, but very uncomfortable at times.

I think I act like I want to be single, but it might just be a plain lie and something I tell myself to fake it until I make it as a single, forty-five-year-old woman who never found love again! Ask me in twenty-four years.

Oh, shit. That's a long time: I'll definitely find love again. Haha! I'm a mess.

Well, here's to my favorite day of the year, and the weirdest one yet. May this year be laid back, fun, and as carefree as possible. As "yes, and" as possible. I'm going to try to stay hopeful and not cynical. Be kind. I'm going to give to my friendships. I'm going to take care of my body physically and emotionally. I'm going to try to give more to K.A.R.L. I'm going to laugh more and keep finding joy in the small things.

Happy April 23rd. This day will always be mine.

I finally feel like myself again. Ah, it feels so good to say and know it's true. Well, I guess I shouldn't say "myself again" because that would imply I've somehow reverted back to some outdated version of myself. (You've seen glimpses of that outdated version and it's pretty cringeworthy.) I finally feel like a version of Kelly I'm proud of, like spending time with, and who cracks me up. I have a freaking blast with myself! Maybe all it takes to fall in love with yourself is a year of quarantining in Imperial, Missouri with infinite hours of alone time! Who knew the answer was so simple?

But I had to put in some serious work, dude. It didn't happen overnight, and "the work" (insert eye roll) will never stop. There's nothing finished here—it's really only just beginning. The fact I have to end this book right here, right now, is crazy because I don't even have time to talk about what I've learned from living in my childhood bedroom for a year during a pandemic and doing my senior year of college from the same laptop I've written a book on. I can't even go there right now. Perhaps it will have to wait for my second book!

The point is I hope to always be growing and evolving, asking hard questions, challenging myself, and opening myself up to opportunities by saying yes to scary things. The quickest way to learn how to swim is to dive into the deep end. (Unless you literally don't know how to swim, then please stay on dry land.)

I've learned "finding yourself" is not really about going out and looking into the world for answers, but going inward and asking hard questions:

Am I selfish? Am I humble? Am I a good friend? What even makes a good friend? How can I be that? Am I capable of more than what I'm doing? Am I scared of something? Am I doubting myself? Am I pursuing what I actually want to be doing?

Maybe I'm a little crazy for being so explicit about it, but there's something really powerful about being intentional with myself and others. I've been writing down manifestos about who I think I am since I was twelve. But if there's anything that reading all of my diary entries has shown me, it's that who we think we are changes because *we* change. And that's okay. Actually, that's freaking awesome!

We're allowed to pivot. We're allowed to go through periods where we don't always have a grasp on who we are. I don't think I'll ever fully understand myself. It's not a requirement, you know! I'm fine with surprising myself every now and then. There's an excitement that goes along with self-discovery! And that goes away once you've cracked the code. It's fun to keep myself on my toes.

Reading these April 23 entries all at once makes it very clear where I messed up, where I got things right, and why things panned out the way they did—so far, at least.

First, I would like to point out a breakup at age twenty probably shouldn't have fucked up my identity the way it did. The problems were literally written out in front of me, but I didn't see them. But no wonder I didn't! I crafted an entire universe around a boy because that's what I thought the answer was; that's what, subconsciously through TV shows, movies, and my surroundings, I've been told to do.

I've spent the last two years beating myself up and being embarrassed that I thought I was going to wind up with my high school sweetheart. But I have to give myself some grace, because it makes sense why I thought that.

My mom got engaged at twenty-one. Most of my aunts and uncles married their high school or college sweethearts. My friends from Imperial—and even high school—are currently getting married and having babies and posting it all over Instagram.

I never watched a TV show about cultivating healthy female friendships. *Are you kidding me?* In Disney princess movies, the answer to happiness is riding off into the sunset with a white guy and leaving all of society behind in the dust! I grew out of those movies and started watching *Mean Girls* and *Legally Blonde* and wanted to be a skinny, blonde, and bitchy sorority girl. Much like my entertainment intake, my reality couldn't pass the Bechdel Test either. Coincidence, hm?

It's no wonder I was putting more energy into a boy than I was into investing in lifelong friendships. I ran to a boyfriend to *escape* female friendships. Even my mother told me to just go get a boyfriend, like it would solve all of my problems. In high school, we didn't know *how* to be good friends. We barely knew how to talk to each other about anything other than boys or talking trash on other girls. I didn't realize, until very recently, friendships are *also* significant relationships that need to be respected, nurtured, and put on a pedestal.

I can't stress how important it is for girls to have their own interests, hobbies, passions, career aspirations, and friendships outside of any romantic relationship. I've spent the last two years building a universe centered around me, my interests, awesome friends, and my crazy family too. It feels fucking great.

I have spent so much time with my parents this year.

(Sorry. I just had to get that out. *Phew.*)

Jesus Christ. They really are nuts. But after writing this book and doing some heavy reflection, I can tell you the best thing my parents have done is believe in me—unconditionally. I have made some pretty wacky decisions, this book being one of them. I think I've changed my major six times, and every single time, I've been met with, "Whatever you gotta do, Kelly. We got you." They've had my back this past year. Even though living with them again has had tremendous ups and downs, I know I will always look back fondly on this unexpected time we had together.

Through all the craziness of 2020 and now 2021 too, I am realizing I have never been more grateful for Imperial, Missouri. The tiny bubble I've spent my entire life resenting has given me the space, safety, and security to embark on the most fulfilling project I've ever taken on: writing this book.

I've turned twenty-two over the course of this project, and I'm inching closer and closer to the edge of adulthood: graduating college, (hopefully) getting a job, and (hopefully) moving to a new city. I've waited my entire life to leave Imperial and move to a big ass city with millions of people and wear nice clothes to a *cool*, *important* job and go to crazy nightclubs with fascinating friends and meet cute boys (men). But now that the time is nearly here, I am scared to leave.

I have fallen in love with this bubble. It's safe and it protects me from Covid-19, government coups, boys, and mean people. The isolation has become so comfortable. I have loved every second of hibernating in my room and writing this book. But now I have to let it go.

As I write this, I can't tell you where I'm going to be a year from now. I can't even tell you where I'm going to be six months from the day I'm writing this. If you told me I'd be in Los Angeles, New York, Berlin, Hong Kong, or Sydney, I'd believe you. That's how much I don't know.

But I've witnessed just enough of life to know things have a way of working themselves out. The Universe, God, or maybe even Stephen Hawking has a plan for us. Despite the little traumas I've endured—from heartbreak to the shit water moat, from people reading my diary to being swung back overseas in the middle of the night, from surviving a global pandemic and living at home in Imperial for my senior year of college—I am okay. In fact, I feel stronger than ever and ready to take these lessons with me on whatever my next journey is because I'm only twenty-two, and I have a lot left to learn.

I can't tell you where I'm going next, but I'll be sure to let you know. We will all get through this (the year, the month, the week, the day) and kick some ass. So let's get this show on the road, baby!

Peace out,

Kelly

Acknowledgments

Kevin & Holly Wiesehan
Marlene McGoff
Don & Nell Wiesehan
Cheryl & Fred Morgan
Sue & Brian Caimi
Blake & Katelyn Caimi
Maria Caimi &
Spencer Carlock
Sandy & Gerard Cahill
Linda & Steve Gray
Erin & Tom Barnowski
Sarah & Andy Sidwell
Laura & Adam Feldmanis
Greg & Debbie Elliott
The Striler Family
The Patterson Family
The Becnel Family
The Bott Family
The Joachimstaler Family

Ellie Phillips
Cecilia Liu
Anastasia Zevan
Emily Geiser
Nathan Shreve
Lauren McGinnis
Andrew Celli
Michael Hofstadter
Sarah Willis
Noa Diamond
Sam Auditore
Jason Lyons
Zachary Stern
Chloe Kilpatrick
Sophie Leib-Neri
David Lee
Adeel Shaikh
Anna Caleca
Josh Rotker

Magdalena Lijowska
Ellen Sheehy
Noah Weiner
Nicole Powell
Katy Fix
Kelli Lepes
Jackie Ballard
Molly Herdlick
Evy Tran
Sophia Mantia
Lucie Donovan
Paige Garozzo
Katie Polizzi
Taylor Hall
Brenna A Brady
Thanh-Thao (Sue) Do
Sydney Moreno
Thomas Mandile
Sneha Chaturvedi
Kennedy Foppe
Emily Williams
Madison Wirth
Angela Simpson
Noor Bekhiet
Gabby Cissi
Elena Quinones
Kristen Doyle
Cole Makuch
Colton Warner

Kaycee Holmes
Cindy Trusler
Isabelle Chickanosky
McClain John
Brooke Adler
Sophie Grigaux
Darrell Barber
Michelle Morgenthal
Giulina Sertl
Madelyn Giegling
Becca Jacobs
Rachel O. Lesinski
Peyton Bonds
Rachael Meyer
Hailey Gilman
Dalia Weinstein
Claire Nelson
Macy Robbins
Laura Glanz
Isabella Vaccaro
Mary Lou Barnes
Michelle Barnes
Madeline Aulbach
Samantha Abel
Rahul Oza
Joseph Souvannarath
Lauren Farkas
Sylvie Skene
Aditya Gandhi

Anna Wurtsbaugh
Grace Panicola
Gillian Laming
Lauren Jin
Leia Barnes
Ginny Sperkowski
Stella Stephanopoulos
Ellie Kenney
Kendall Edgren
Stephanie Ebert
Nicole Gaudin
Maddy Rettig
Eric Koester
Lucas Dionisopoulos
Folake Ayiloge
Jessica Almgren-Bell
Meghan Jones
Jack Phillips
Anne Kramer
Alexandra Boehm
Sahil Patel
Natalie Hall
Jamey Briscoe
Sofia Burnett
Jen Rustige
Tyler Leonard

Tara Satnick
Natalia Wright
Terri Wilson
Merry Kweiter
Elizabeth Feldman
Emma Harrison
Nora Brooks
Margie Palazzolo
Sophia Goldman
Allison Portelance
Cameron Ippolito
Grace Johnston
Claire Murphy
Irene Searles
Abigale Rudolph
Ariel Grosfeld
Marci Damiano
Lexie Schomaker
Jordan A. Schroeder
Abby Ohlendorf
Sammi O'Reilly
Isabel Edison
Corky Ribakoff
Nicole Soell
Gina Oesterlei
Elisabeth Middleton

Made in the USA
Middletown, DE
12 May 2021